SEA~COUNTRY

Exploring Thames Estuary By-ways
Under Sail

by

TONY SMITH

with photographs by the author

Lodestar Books

Published 2014 by
Lodestar Books
71 Boveney Road, London, SE23 3NL, United Kingdom

www.lodestarbooks.com

A CIP catalogue record for this book
is available from the British Library

ISBN 978-1-907206-25-2

Typeset by Lodestar Books in Equity

Printed in Spain by Graphy Cems, Navarra

All papers used by Lodestar Books
are sourced responsibly

Contents

1

Creek-Sailing

A LOOK ON THE CHART of the East Coast shows us that there are a dozen or so tidal rivers that indent it from North Foreland, Kent in the south, up to Orfordness, Suffolk in the north. This wider area is called the Thames Estuary, a vast triangular, shoal-studded stretch of water off the south-east of England and in the southern corner of the North Sea, encompassing approximately 400 square miles. Inside these rivers can be found hundreds of smaller creeks, some of them resembling small rivers in themselves, where relatively safe sailing can be found.

My 16ft 6in miniature gaff cutter *Shoal Waters* is kept on a drying mud mooring in a picturesque creek in the county of Essex. The Essex coastline is approximately 350 miles long. Not a straight line of coast but a ragged, low, marshy coast profusely indented by the sea's tentacles that have spread vein-like inland, forming a modern day creek-sailor's heaven.

There is evidence that ancient communities once dwelt on the shores here gathering salt, and Roman Legions, religious saints, raiding Vikings and 17th century smugglers have all left their mark here too. The late 19th and early 20th century saw the heyday of the ubiquitous flat-bottomed Thames sailing barge, built to transport goods around the shallow East Coast and serve farm wharves that sit at the head of many creeks. They too, along with other abandoned 'hulks', have in one way or another left their mark on this salty corner of Britain. For the potential visitor it is useful to know that some creeks reveal themselves at or near low water when they become shallow gut-ways that interweave a muddy estuary. Others are saltmarsh-fringed, narrow and twisting channels that can only be navigated around the high water mark. Some are a mixture of the two. There are many terms used to describe the form of sailing that takes place in these murky waters such as ditch-crawling, mud-hopping, creek-crawling to name a few, but I like to refer to this perhaps somewhat esoteric activity as creek-sailing. Creek-sailing can often cover the gamut of small boat cruising. In my local estuary for example, the River Blackwater in Essex, there are 64 named creeks and dozens more without names that I know of and have explored. Nearby and within an easy day's sailing there are the Rivers Colne, Crouch and Roach which have their own creeks and offshoots that can all be reached on the next high tide. One of the prettiest little creeks I have adventured in along the whole East Coast is the delightful and somewhat treacherous Fingringhoe Creek, also known as the Roman River, off the River Colne. This creek begins with a huge mud shoal on the first bend and continues to try and trip you up every turn it makes through some of Essex's hillier sea-country, and the reward at its head is to be taken back in time into a Victorian country setting by a magnificently restored and converted tide mill and granary building. A challenge that is hard to resist.

However, there comes a time when even the most avid creek sailor might wish to extend his cruising ground and explore creeks in other areas, such as the delightfully-named Bedlams Bottom in Funton Creek in the River Medway estuary, or venture up to Arthur Ransome's Secret Water in the Walton Backwaters and test one's wit in the narrow waters of Beaumont Cut. Into the River Orwell even, or that mud-filled outpost that is Johnny All Alone Creek, in the River Stour. Tackle the shifting sand-bars of Suffolk's River Deben and River Ore where you could be late on the tide to visit the Deben's 'Early Creek' or that well known anchorage in the Ore's Butley Creek where a boat arrives on the tide for a day at anchor and stays for a week—or two!

For the small-boat sailor, moving along the coast between these rivers does require more careful planning and wise use of weather and tides, and it is more often than not on these occasions when there are white-knuckle moments as you head out of the confines and safety of the local estuary to venture along the open coast before heading inland again for your targeted creek. Having made your early arrival there is the excitement of anticipation, as your chosen creek slowly becomes navigable by the mystery of the tides.

For the most part the creek environment is remote, uncluttered and peaceful, with a soundtrack of wild nature. The creeks can be looked upon as capillaries of the sea too, for they are full of nutrients which wading birds feed on and are where edible marsh samphire (sea asparagus), sea purslane, oysters and winkles grow in abundance. This is something that even the Romans knew about, for it is widely thought they too used the muddy creeks to grow oysters. While exploring in the majority of creeks the creek-sailor finds his way not by navigation buoys but by sensual feeling of the shallow depths and eyeing the eerie, ghostly-looking withies that inhabit them. These withies are in the main cut-down branches that mark oyster layings or mud shoals that would otherwise trap an unwary skipper. But often they can be more sinister-looking metal affairs that could put a hole your boat, and mark only what the person who put them there knows.

After the Second World War and when more reliable roads were built the coastal transportation of goods by sea declined rapidly, and many an old boat was run up a creek and abandoned to become at one with the marshes. Many of these wrecks, hulks as they are known on the East Coast, still reside in quiet corners of creeks where they never fail to intrigue the passing sailor with their blistering, twisted and splintered timbers, or rusting iron—history you can touch. Every creek has something different about it though. It may be a particular bird species, a wreck, deep mud, a shingle beach, a wharf, trees, buildings, a ghost even. Whatever it is they all have one thing inherently in common, which is the salty tide that flows in and out twice in every twenty four hours.

It all adds up to an interesting and varied cruising ground for the small boat sailor, and today there are thousands of boaters based on this shallow coast who have access to the myriad of tiny creeks; yet still many creeks remain uncharted, quiet and forgotten backwaters. These are the realm of the three-feet-depth waterman, perhaps the ultimate domain of the self-respecting ditch-sliders, shallow sailors, thin water sailors, short-sea-farers and ditch-crawlers.

An intriguing sight for the uninitiated is to see the skipper of a small cruiser stabbing ferociously into the depths a garden cane, in search of more water; the stick is waved almost as a magic wand to produce an even murkier, pasty swirl, to take him even further into his idyll. The knee-deep sailor carries an armoury of hand tools to help him in his never ending quest for that thinner piece of water, near-dry sailing, giving entrance to the thickest of muds or the most sheltered of sandbanks where no other boat has ventured for decades, if at all.

The auxiliary, if of any help thus far, has long been clipped in its up position and forgotten. If one has well-fitted bulkhead compasses they are now next to useless, but a snatched bearing taken quickly by hand is often fruitful. 12-volt cabling sending haywire depth signals is of no use to this skipper, but the cane does not lie to those who dwell in water of 3ft or less. In deeper than 'stick' water he sinks the lead. But here and now the skipper is at the very pinnacle of his chosen art with both hands on; close-quarter working with bean-stick sounding-cane bought in bulk from the garden centre, as he can get through many in a season. He stands thrashing to his favoured side, not clumsily but with a well-practised setting of the stick at precise moments to read accurately, either from the knuckle in the cane or from the white painted markers set at foot intervals. He alternates this cane wizardry with powerful strokes of the short oar to stay in full command of his little vessel.

Every now and then a short pause is made as the mud below grips his keel. Mainsail is now lowered, or taken in, with sail ties clove-hitched; the jib can come in a little too, or stay set just in case. Suddenly a comprehensive array of tea-making facilities takes over the main focus for a short while, and soon enough the little boat wobbles back to life. If not already worn, water-boots or thigh-waders are now donned in case there is an urgent need to hop overboard to free the boat. Frantic jabbing movements are made with the 15ft-long quant pole either from the side decks or cockpit, often now to no avail as things have become 'real dirty', and only those few of a certain disposition press ahead, for they sense that the reward for their efforts is near. The rudder is now tied in its up position; the centreboard is fully up and cleated tight. A stiff jerking pull from side to side with the tiller in what remains of the 'water due', and the rudder throws thick ooze sloshing along the raised bank.

At this point the boat is now laying in resemblance to a stranded sea-bass or mullet with her rudder hanging next to useless. But all is not lost, as this was his intention, he has achieved his aim, he is at the limit, the extremes of his salt-water habitat and surrounded by the glory of man and woman that is sea-country.

Immediately the greeting call of the reed warbler rings out and redshank scurry along the mud. The ever-ready skipper cleans the tools that have become extension to his creek-sailor's arms (now there's a name for a pub) as scent of mud drifts across creek and marshland.

Once you have experienced cruising in these waters it can be difficult to sail anywhere else, for the seaweed-filled, saltmarsh-fringed murky coast has a draw of its own. Elsewhere seas are bluer, with whiter waves and warmer waters, but can they ever equal this brown shoal-studded, mud-lined creek haven, where one can run aground at will and put the kettle on for a brew?

My collection of close-quarter creek-sailing tools includes a variety of paddles and oars and bamboo sounding-cane 'sticks'. Even the boat-hook is marked up to double as a sounder. Over the years I have got through many sticks, through them falling overboard when heeling in rough weather, or through heat-of-the-moment carelessness. Often time is spent searching over covered ground in search of a favoured stick that has served so well. It's always with a feeling of elation, such as when scoring a goal in football, that you happen to find them again. I have played about with sticking pieces of lead or taping a thick piece of cork to them to stop them sinking through the really soft stuff. I have also tried with bits of line as a handle to hook onto a part of the boat, but it's not necessary.

Classic East Coast mud is as pure as nature intended. Learn to love this stuff. The sounding-cane gives reliable readings when prodding and the technique is to sense the bottom with 'feel'. Surprisingly enough a thin bean stick stops an inch or so in when under its own inertia. Trying to weigh up the bottom texture and depth before attempting to cross it on foot is a good practice. Wading through deep mud is never an exact science, but sweet and 'smelly' in its most endearing sense it is. I guess correctly (sometimes) that mud would go at least knee deep and be a patch of welly-stealer, a Dick Turpin of the low tide sea-ways. Here is a substrate where maintaining movement and agility is everything; a pair of wooden splatchers would slow down the sink effect considerably too. Then again, play safe and find a harder patch nearby.

A minimal draft of 12 inches allows one to dwell in the habitats only accessible by wading birds. However, it is no secret that a boat drawing four feet should be able to reach most places in the estuary, even if only at the top of a spring tide.

2

The Smaller Boat

WHAT IS THE ATTRACTION with small boats and cruising? 'Less is more' is a term sometimes mentioned in small-boat cruising circles. I understand this term to mean you get more enjoyment from cruising in a small boat than you would in a big boat. The reality of this cannot be true, as the man or woman who owns a 200ft yacht, fully crewed, and cruises the world's remote tropical islands is sure to be enjoying the experience. Therefore 'more' must mean something other than a material gain in cabin size, sail area, or length of waterline. Exactly what 'more' is will vary with each individual boat owner but if we put aside any financial constraints, why do many of us enjoy owning a small cruiser? For the purpose of this chapter I will refer to a small boat as being an open boat or cabin cruiser of around 20ft or less that has restricted headroom and cabin space. Cost is certainly a factor for most people when buying a boat, but this is only one reason people buy small, as I know of very wealthy people who choose to own a small boat.

If we accept there is only one potential negative of owning a small boat, and that is its limited space inside, we quickly move on to take a look at a few of the many pluses: the ease of handling when sailing; the ease of lowering and raising the mast; the ability to sail single handed; the enjoyment of being on a big sea in such a small craft; the ability to reach the most awkward of tight places and waterways;

the trailability, the cosiness of the cabin; the less time spent maintaining the boat and less equipment needing to be replaced.

The fun that is there to be had with a small boat is just the same in a £1,000 GRP standard build as a £25,000 hand built wooden classic. The only difference I can see being mainly cosmetic. Other more meaningful reasons to own a small boat may be to limit your carbon footprint, or to cleanse your spirit with minimalist delight, by making do with a small cabin space, in which there is crouching room only and no running water or toilet facilities. Perhaps to the yachtsman who cruises in a bigger boat with space below for a six berth caravan all draped in net curtains that can twitch in cul-de-sacked marinas, this small boating caper might seem a hardship beyond belief, but it is only after trying something for a period of time that we realise how we can do without many things in life we have come to rely on, and how refreshing this can be.

Cooking on a small boat presents a challenge that can be a pain or a pleasure. This is one area that I feel makes a big impact on the comfort level felt by the small boat skipper. To arrange a small boat's galley to some kind of order could well involve taking ideas from that 30 ft yacht, or the 'kitchen indoors'. I delight in seeing how people deal with this in such creative ways.

There is another attraction to the small boat rarely mentioned, that has similarities to the garden shed. Every man or woman who has a little shed at the bottom of the garden uses it for a million and one things, but one of them is escaping to a small world where everything seems to be manageable and in its place. The basic 6ft x 4ft wooden shed has to be the ultimate in minimalism. But I've even seen net curtains screening tiny shed windows, and heavy duty electric cables plugged into the house fuse box and disguised under cabbage and runner bean leaves, fed to wired-in light bulbs and electric boiling kettles and the like; yes you know who you are!

For some, this shed effect is felt in the small boat, but with the freedom to roam the waves of an estuary or river, or a length of coastline, before pulling the boat up a peaceful beach and camping out under the stars. This is a tonic hard to beat and is another major draw for the small-boat cruiser. I've yet to enter a marina in *Shoal Waters* while cruising; in fact the closest we came was mooring alongside the pontoons in Brightlingsea Creek for an Old Gaffers' rally. It's not that I object to the idea of paying for an overnight berth, they just don't feature in my itinerary, for my boat is a creature of the marshes, and with her flat bottom lives happily on a drying mud anchorage. Most of the creeks I like to visit are pretty remote so I try to be as self-sufficient as possible, and always carry spare gas, a sack of tea bags, and a selection of tinned food and powdered milk which doesn't go off.

Shoal Waters' minimalist cabin space has full sitting headroom, and dressing or changing of clothes is done while lying down or in the canvas cockpit tent. The fully-equipped galley is to port with kitchen utensils and tins of food stored in a milk crate which has a plywood top doubling up as a table. The centreboard case is curved but while at anchor this is surmounted by a flat piece of wood which creates more usable surface. The bread larder is on the port side as are the stove and full tea making facilities which are ready to hand from the cockpit, making brewing up while under way an easy procedure. There are three non-spill open lockers above on both sides for placing odds and ends like keys and hand torches and there is an open bookshelf on the port side just forward of these and an open shelf on the starboard side used for storing charts and pilotage notes. All surfaces are wash-clean varnish and the luxury sleeping arrangements are to starboard, these are made of four inch thick foam as is the red cushioned lounge area. The small cabin caters for single-handing quite comfortably but an extra berth is formed in the forward port side if the starboard birth is slid aft two feet. Spare tools used for close quarter creek-sailing such as paddles and sounding canes are stored forward.

Under way the boom crutch is folded away and stored under the starboard cockpit seat and accessed from the cabin. The folding slats for the cockpit tent are stored here too along with a satchel of spare ropes and anything else not needed to hand that I tend to stuff under there out of the way. Water is dispensed from four 5-litre plastic containers that sit on the starboard side under the bridge deck, and washing and shaving is done in a small plastic bowl.

Cooking is done on the single gas stove and pots and pans are stored under the hinged wooden worktops. I carry two kettles onboard; one is also used to continue the ship's long tradition of cooking steak and kidney pies in.

Carrying all this cruising equipment means she is perhaps not as quick as she could be, but then this is not at the top of my list of what makes a decent cruiser. What she does have is character by the bucket-load, and she is without a doubt a joy to sail, making an average of three knots with her gaff cutter rig. Her tiny blade of a jib sits on the end of her bowsprit and her small staysail is fixed to a stem-head gammon iron, both sails being furled on Wykeham-Martin gear. The loose-footed mainsail has two sets of reefing points and is attached at the luff by four mast hoops, and controlled by the centre mainsheet which I prefer. The mast sits in a tabernacle so it can be lowered for bridges when penetrating deep inland.

I'm fortunate to have sailed a previous boat, of the same size, with Bermudan rig and with gaff rig and found the difference negligible in the places where I spend most of my time. But in answer to friends who were intrigued to gain a measure of *Shoal Waters*' performance, and due to the fact I am a sociable guy, I was persuaded to enter a local club cruiser race during the summer of 2012 which involved two events, sailed against three Bermudan-rig Leisure 17s, a Hunter Sonata and a Cornish Shrimper. Now, I am not a racing man and looked on it as a light-hearted bit of sailing fun I could take part in before I took off on another cruise; but fully laden with cruising gear she never came last over the line, so the club gave her the handicap of the Leisure 17, which meant she came second and third respectively out of the two races.

In 2013 *Shoal Waters* turned 50 years old, an event that coincided with the Old Gaffers Association 50th birthday celebrations which we took part in. *Shoal Waters* was one of the original boats at the first East Coast gathering held in 1963 inside the River Blackwater, so it was my pleasure to be able to take her to this special event, this time in Brightlingsea Creek off the River Colne, where she achieved second place in her class.

What has surprised me with her is how she manages to sail in the lightest of airs. One example of this was sailing up the River Deben in Suffolk with hardly any breeze at all, though I did have the magic carpet that is a fair tide. Methodically I plodded on while another craft that by then I was creeping up on suddenly downed sails and fired up the outboard, disappearing out of sight. I couldn't give up as I had no engine, instead I played my trump card and set the small topsail—a simple matter of lowering the gaff and bending it on as it is left permanently attached to and rolled around its bamboo yard and stored in the cabin. With topsail hoisted we kept moving at barely a knot, two at most, with just enough way to steer us through the moored craft at Felixstowe Ferry and Ramsholt that are rather densely packed in some parts. A few hours later I sailed past the same chap, who by now was sitting on a buoy at Waldringfield, about six miles upriver. As I passed he called over "She sails well." She sails well enough, I thought, but I like to think it was more of a case of determination of the skipper and not giving in at the first sign of being becalmed.

Other than the sounding cane and binoculars I find the most important piece of kit I carry is the 17lb fisherman-style anchor, which sits in readiness permanently on the bow. This is used many times during a day's creek sailing as I often stop at the head of some tranquil backwater, and it has also saved me from the suck and pull of the tide while cruising around the sandbanks and swatchways out in the Thames Estuary.

For navigation I use the ship's WWII landing craft compass, for which I have a red night light, as well as a hand held Sestrel for taking bearings; and for the most part I use small Admiralty charts and Ordnance Survey maps for passage planning; but most of my cruising is near land where pilotage, the ship's barometer and one's senses of sight and feel rule. I love the feeling of liberation which results from sailing with these most basic of navigation aids.

I do allow a couple of modern gadgets on board though. One is a basic handheld GPS which I sometimes carry when heading out of a river in the hope that if I were to get lost in fog I could get a position; but I find it far more useful as a log for working out arrival times for a particular point on route, and it has been a useful speed indicator for an optimally set rig. The other gadget is a handheld VHF radio. Perhaps a vital safety aid today for anyone putting to sea, especially if one sails alone, this is great for planning your next move after receiving the local area three-hourly weather broadcasts by the coastguard.

3

The Essex Loop

WHEN I RAN THE LITTLE GREEN CUTTER *Shoal Waters* onto her trailer at the back end of 2011, it was the end to a glorious first year of sailing with my new boat. I had already decided to trailer her home for the winter layup, and all being good I would launch her into the upper reaches of the River Stort the following Easter. The Stort forms part of an ancient trade route to and from all ports of the world, and the prospect of taking its course all the way to London via the River Lee and the newly-built Olympic stadium—to then pass through the historic Bow Locks and navigate the tidal Bow Creek, and up the East Coast via the mighty Thames—made an irresistible prospect.

Not only that, but this trip would be a double win as the boat would end up on her mooring at Goldhanger Creek in the River Blackwater by the end of the seven-day trip. Having been born an east-ender, I had spent much time on the banks of the lower Lee and the Thames in my early years, so this would be a journey of personal significance too.

To sail these rivers in the true sense of the word in a mast-rigged seagoing cabin cruiser takes some determination, as there are more than 100 low bridges to 'shoot' along the inland leg of the journey, as well as 29 locks to pass through. My aim therefore was to sail if and when possible using mainsail or 'bridgesail,' but I could also use all man-powered methods such as paddles, quant pole and 'bow-hauling', ie towing, using the towpath to literally pull the boat along by hand.

Similarly, the cargo barges that the River Stort was dug by hand for in 1769 would have been pulled along by horse at walking pace. It was not unusual for these commercial boats to use a small bridgesail in the form of a simple sprit rig set on a short mast to help them on their way from one end of the river to the other.

The working barges and tow horses that would visit the quayside in the market town of Bishop's Stortford, Hertfordshire, to take malt and other cargos up and down the river have long since vanished, along with a way of life. Jackson Wharf was named after Sir George Jackson, who later changed his name to Dukkets; he helped finance the completion of the Stort Navigation, was a friend of the intrepid explorer Captain Cook, who had homes here and in London. Cook named Port Jackson (Sydney Harbour), in Australia, and Point Jackson in New Zealand after Jackson.

Today, modern flats sit at the old wharves beside the river in its upper reaches around the town. It is as if the town has turned its back on the waterway, much preferring the roads and railways that pass literally yards away in some instances, and often almost parallel to the river on its way south. This situation is mirrored up and down the country on many of our inland waterways. The river now lays quiet, forgotten even, draped in many places with lush green willow trees and hovered over by colourful kingfishers: it's a place of incredible beauty. The River Stort—and to a large extent the River Lee—have become wildlife oases, and for many people somewhere to seek sanctuary from the busy world we now live in.

The Stort finds its source coming from fields above the Essex village of Clavering, and the Lee begins just above the Bedfordshire

Jackson Wharf, Bishop's Stortford, taken by Charles Stock in 1982

Jackson Wharf today

town of Luton. On the journey southwards the rivers pass many former watermills and malting buildings, natural marshland and flat meads. Long-time favourites of narrow boat and canoe enthusiasts, these rivers have tended to be somewhat overlooked by cruising sailors—which, for me, merely adds to their appeal.

I opened the companionway and peered out across the marshland of Little Hallingbury to an old watermill. Even if it was a cold, damp and cloudy start to the new day, my spirits lifted at the sight of the mill sitting at the foot of a hill in a valley, strikingly similar to the one on the upper River Stour in Suffolk, made famous by the artist Constable. I buzzed like a bee at the fact I had opened my cruising account for 2012 and was with the boat again in such a wonderful countryside setting. I'd launched the boat from her trailer into the river the day before at the privately-owned Kecksys Farm on the outskirts of Sawbridgeworth. For the shoal draught trailer-sailer owner, the little slip here is a rare amenity in these parts. The river itself borders East Hertfordshire and West Essex; and for anyone who may think of Essex as a flat and somewhat barren land, this is one part of the county where that myth is truly blown away.

From a tidal sea-sailor's perspective, the stillness of the water was apparent immediately after launching. There is no urgency as there can be when dealing with a tideway; the first two or three paddle-strokes take some effort, but then the boat glides almost effortlessly under her own inertia and one or two occasional strokes keep her in motion.

A wonderful time was had on the Stort with my friend Brian and my son and daughter joining me over four days to crew, taking it in turns bow-hauling, helming and working the locks. 'Grip the monkey's fist and lean slightly forward with the rope over one shoulder,'

I yelled to my son Harry. He looked bemused at first but was soon enjoying the novelty of bow-hauling a cruising yacht.

All too soon we'd covered the length of the river and we parted at the last lock, where I paddled on into the sunset to moor alongside the towpath and enjoy the night under a clear sky in this rural utopia.

The following day called for an early start: not only was I now single-handed, but I also had eleven locks to pass through on my journey south along the River Lee. The Lee, considerably wider than the Stort, is known as London's other river and was busy with commercial traffic until the 1970s, serving the many timber wharves that once lined its banks.

I was wide awake by the time I'd passed through Fieldes Lock; the further downstream I reached, the more urbanized the waterway became. However, it struck me that barely another boat was using the waterway, although a hive of industry hummed just beyond the fences and walls above the banks. Many towpaths on the Lee are now lined with liveaboard barges, a number of which are permanently cruising—moving every two weeks to a new mooring. I can recall that the banks here were deserted back in the 1980s, other than for the odd steel lighter sat beside empty, overhanging wharves.

A very active day lay ahead and the next lock was soon in sight, so the task of working the lock gates was put into practice again. I relish the physical element that this form of cruising has. Typically there's an hour or two of paddling or towing, culminating in heaving pairs of giant pivoting gates across the river, having to move from one side of the lock via a bridge to the other, and back again to then wind ferociously on the windlass to open ground paddles and release an incredible force of water. I set the bridgesail to drift along from Tottenham Hale to where I spent the night at Springfield and the Lee Valley Marina moorings. It was great to be able to use the showers after five nights afloat.

The next morning, I set off downriver at 0500. Graffiti decorated the old warehouses, and new towpaths had been built in many places. Bridges gleamed with fresh paintwork and workboats seemed to be all about the river from Lea Bridge Road down to Hackney Marshes, which could well have been in the countryside looking from my position in the centre of the river.

After Marshgate Bridge the sun beamed down as I raised *Shoal Waters'* mast to sail alongside the Olympic stadium, revelling in its scale. My booking with the lock keeper to pass through the tidal Bow Locks was at 3pm, so I nipped into the Hertford Union Canal in pouring rain before heading back down the Lee. With 50 minutes to go I tied up at the historic Three Mills for bread and milk at Tesco, just over the bridge. The rain continued teeming down for the last leg; *Shoal Waters* was cruising at a genteel 1.2 knots, powered by the now favoured duck canvas bridgesail, and I savoured my first sighting of Canary Wharf tower and the distinctive Bow Locks with their 1930s cast concrete footbridge.

With superb timing, the lock gates opened and the keeper ushered me into the right-hand lock. To pass through the locks you need a working VHF radio, your boat insurance documents and the appropriate Rivers Licence, which the lock keeper asked to see. Before locking out the keeper advised me to call London VTS on Ch14 to warn them of my intended outbound passage down the creek. This turned out to be a vitally important detail, because the creek was in constant use by tugs towing football-pitch-sized lighters up and down for the Olympic site. Once locked out I had to wait against a nearby wharf wall for an hour while two tugs with tows passed by.

Near the Olympic Stadium on the Lee Navigation

London's only lighthouse, at Trinity Buoy Wharf

The Thames Barrier

The Queen Elizabeth II Bridge across the Thames at Dartford

I was early on the flood tide, but the sun shone over flat calm water as I chugged down the creek. The inland waterways are a tonic and I enjoyed the two inland rivers immensely, but was glad to be back in the salt and thrashing with my sounding cane into the soft mud a few feet below.

Bow Creek is in effect the lower River Lee, here somewhat confusingly spelt 'Lea.' The creek is shouldered by heavy cast concrete quays and is bridged by huge iron structures bearing the full weight of East London's industrial traffic.

Above the wharves, Dockland skyscrapers disappeared behind misty clouds. Gulls cruised above the River Thames and the O2 Arena was ahead as I pulled into the wall behind two former Trinity House light vessels at Trinity Buoy Wharf, the mouth of Bow Creek. I climbed over the wall and found the wharf manager, who kindly permitted me to stay alongside for the night. I visited London's only lighthouse; this was used by Trinity as a testing light but now houses Longplayer, a fascinating music of chimes and bell sounds that was started in the Millennium year and which will play nonstop for 1,000 years.

Before dark I raised the mast for the final time and fully rigged the boat, checking everything over in readiness for sea sailing. Two hours before high tide the following morning, *Shoal Waters* sailed out of Bow Creek and into the mighty London River, under the new cablecar structure and towards the Thames Barrier. I called the barrier on the VHF radio and requested passage through. 'Use Bravo Gate which is lit by two green lights,' came the reply. Suddenly thick fog groped upriver from the east, causing high anxiety aboard *Shoal Waters*. Where was Bravo Gate with the green lights? It eventually loomed out of the fog and we passed safely and were soon well under way, still in thick fog with all navigation lights on. Below Woolwich the commercial traffic eased until the QE2 Bridge came into view, and then Tilbury Docks on the north bank. This was the domain of the big boys—huge container ships shuffling their way about the river, and at the same time the wind went north by east and drew me away from the lee shore of the starboard side and towards the dock, which required caution.

I was soon charging past Gravesend and Bawley Bay, an area beside the little St Andrew's Church where many shrimp boats once moored. The estuary began to widen and I found myself working the sounding cane across Blyth Sands and eyeing up the snug little Egypt Bay for the coming night, keeping well out of the way of shipping that kept rolling on by, heading upriver.

The forecast came in of a north-easterly Force 4 or 5, increasing to 6 later, with strong wind warnings to follow. This had me scurrying off to the Leigh Deposit Buoy and battling north-eastward, out over the flood toward the Shoebury Beacon. This was a seemingly impossible task against wind and tide, but I needed to be in the safety of the River Roach by nightfall. I cut inside the wreck of the Mulberry harbour Phoenix unit to be in shoal water. The wind was building all too quickly, enabling a battling beat, not out to the Shoebury—that was now beyond reach—but a few tacks across the fabled sands gave me some hard-earned ground, and I could point north to pass close to the Inner Shoebury Beacon, where many obstructions lay.

I listened for any sounds coming from the plate, but we were clear: I could now ease the sheets a little and reach northward across the Maplin Sands in 4ft of water. A hectic time with the sounding cane found me the withies that mark the deeper water of Havengore Creek, and the reward now lay ahead. The sun was coming down, and with a following wind I sailed into Havengore Creek for the

1838 high tide. The bridge-keeper raised the bridge in good time and *Shoal Waters* glided past into the sanctuary of Narrow Cuts and up through Middleway and Yokesfleet Creeks, where seals followed us into Devil's Reach. The sound of terns calling faded and I was soon out of the Roach and at Shore Ends in the River Crouch by 2130. "That's enough sailing for today," I said to myself, and dropped the hook. I hadn't been long settled in the bunk when I was awoken by an RNLI RIB searchlight. They asked if I was alright, and enquired if I'd seen a man in the sea?

The following morning I left at high water for the near 10-mile beat up the coast. To avoid the worst of the choppy seas at the mouth of the Crouch I cunningly guided *Shoal Waters* from Holliwell Point across the shallow Ray Sand like a slithering sand-eel.

Sea conditions were pretty lively and I felt scared for a while, so I hove to and pulled down a reef. I passed the two new safe water marks in the swatchway a couple of hours later and suddenly things began to calm down again, encouraging me to shake out the reef and unfurl the jib. The remote chapel of St Peter-on-the-Wall, built in AD654 by St Cedd, came into view and soon I was heading up the Blackwater once more. I enjoyed some fantastic sailing to scrape onto my drying mud mooring in Goldhanger Creek, stepping ashore to end a wonderful 'Essex Loop' cruise.

The Broomway

I HAVE SAILED OVER THE BROOMWAY on many occasions in two to four feet of water, and have walked parts of it at low water, but had never completed its full six-mile length from Wakering Stairs to Fisherman's Head. So I decided to leave the boat on her mooring and drive down to Great Wakering to undertake the walk in its entirety. The Broomway has been a means of access to Foulness Island for centuries, possibly even being used by the Romans, but what attracts me to this by-way is its location; the wild expanse of the Maplin Sands gives me an awareness of our insignificance on this planet, in a place where my thoughts can run free. There are two sea-forts visible away to the east, and gunning lookout towers are clearly visible along the shore of Foulness Island to the west, so even here our capacity to do harm is evident.

The term 'broomway' originates from when the islanders placed posts or 'brooms' at intervals along the sands to mark the route, and travelled along it on foot or cart. Today the way is largely unmarked and one needs to have a good navigational sense, and a sound knowledge of the tides, to traverse the way in both directions in one dry 'window'. The sands can be soft underfoot, causing fatigue and consequent problems.

Once past the obstacle of the firing range, which may have red flags raised closing access to the sands, one needs to allow for roughly six hours of continual walking for the two-way journey. The tide can appear suddenly. If I can offer one word of advice it would be prepare yourself physically by doing a walk across soft terrain for five or six hours in one session, a couple of weeks beforehand, to see how your body reacts to it, then you will have the confidence that you can endure the journey. The last thing you would want while out on the sands is muscle cramp, in fact any unforeseen mishap disabling you, for the tide waits for no-one and your calls for help are highly likely to go unheard. When your preparation is done and you take the first step onto the sand at Wakering Stairs, embrace the moment for it is truly magical.

4

Cockles at Leigh

DOWN WHERE THE THAMES IS WIDE and the Essex and Kent shores are barely visible from one side to the other through a milky haze, a salty half-tide gutway can be found with enough water for a small boat to cut a path north-westward through Chalkwell Oaze mudflats, where a scattering of craft lie wedged to dry mud moorings in a restless wait for the tide to return. We are in Leigh Swatch, just south of the Crowstone, an ancient marker that pairs with London Stone, across the estuary due south at the mouth of Yantlet Creek, to mark the seaward limit of jurisdiction over fishing rights once held over the Thames by the City of London.

A nice run in from here has us making a sharp turn north followed shortly after by a 90 degree turn to port which has the creek trickling west again—past *Wilton*, an ex-Royal Navy mine hunter, now home to the Essex Yacht Club—until we find the drowned-twice-daily Leigh Marsh off Two Tree Island just to the southwest. But the creek leads ever closer toward the Leigh shore until it arrives at the foot of a rising cliff at Bell Wharf where there is soft golden sand, and Leigh-On-Sea Sailing Club can be found in a former railway station building. Here we are at Old Leigh and in Leigh Creek, which for centuries was a waterside fishing community. On the cliffs and hills of modern Leigh sits a bustling commuter town just 45 minutes from London's Fenchurch Street Station, but its links to fishing,

well documented from the 15th century, and traceable for almost a thousand years, are evident in the bygone cobbled alleyways and the handful of local families which still work from this little estuary port. And though the boats and equipment used by today's fishermen are a world away from the sail-powered boats of the 1800s, we are fortunate on the East Coast that many enthusiasts keep former local working boats sailing in a colourful display of living history.

While the early 20th century saw the shrimp fishing industry flourish at Leigh, it is perhaps cockles for which the town has become most famous. On crisp sunny mornings the cockle boats would leave this little estuary port at the call of the tide, and with barely enough water to keep them off the deep muddy sides of the creek, toddling their way down to the Swatch and out onto the Maplins in a stream of boats resembling a trail of worker ants. With their shallow draft they aimed to ground on the sands with just enough time for the men to hop over the side in waders, to labour in a bent-over stance for around four hours gathering the cockles by hand with a rake, then filling the boat's hold before floating off home again on the returning tide.

Leigh Creek flows close to the promenade wall at Alley Dock and Theobalds Wharf, where at Mike's Boatyard lines of fidgeting dunlin stand guard over their patch, behind them a pub or two, *The Mayflower*, *Ye Old Smack* and *The Peter Boat*. The Endeavour Trust's restored cockler *Endeavour* is moored just off the promenade here. She was the last wooden fishing boat built at Leigh with an auxiliary rig that could enable her to work under sail. She is also a Dunkirk 'Little Ship,' being one of six fishing boats out of Leigh that took part in the evacuation of troops. The other five were *Defender*, *Letitia*, *Reliant*, *Resolute*, and *Renown* which tragically was lost, with all crew, to a mine on her return journey. It was while under enemy

The modern cockler *Renown IV* in Leigh Creek

Vacated cockle shells

fire that those brave crews in their Leigh cockle boats were able to transport many hundreds of troops each, from the hazardous shallows out to deeper water where the larger ships awaited them. The Renown was built in 1928 by Hayward's of Southend and was the first of four Osborne-owned boats to take the same name.

If we follow the creek a little further westward we find the *Renown IV*, the successor to those early wooden craft, owned and still fished for cockles by the Osborne family, who have shrimped and netted whitebait from Leigh for five generations. A collection of quaint two-up, two-down fishermen's cottages are sat around Victoria, Strand and Billet Wharves, and Osborne's Café which is sited in an 18th century stable mews once used for horses and carts associated with the adjacent Crooked Billet public house. Behind the wharves and buildings a skinny cobblestone road, the High Street, finds its way parallel to the creek until it joins Cockleshed Row, where boarded and painted wooden sheds tempt passers-by with a display of cockles, crabs, whelks, mussels and winkles; to the rear the sheds peer down over ten-foot-high mounds of cockle shells that await disposal on local farm fields and paths. The shells are what remains from the cooking and cleaning process; the flesh is separated and given a series of washes to clear any remaining grit, ready to be eaten fresh, or frozen for later.

Opposite the cockle sheds the creek forks south into the Gas House Cut and the back of Two Tree Island, where *Navigator* and *Souvenir*, a couple of old-timers from the former fleet of Leigh Bawley boats, sit half buried in saltmarsh. Another boat leaning against *Navigator* is *Thames Server*, an old lifeboat used to run pilots out from Southend Pier to incoming ships. The creek then flows on to Leigh Motor-Boat Club with its own slipway, its clubhouse in the form of MV *Lea*, a barge brought from Holland for the purpose, and its many boats cushioned in mud, up to the road bridge onto the island. If we pass the last cockle shed the creek trickles into an inlet where dozens of dinghies bob to the tide, kept by the Belton Way Small Craft Club, a band of the saltiest small-boat mariners you are likely to encounter on the whole East Coast, who have a delightful shed with veranda suspended over a tiny strip of beach. I had a cuppa with Brum, and Mick, a large man sporting a woollen hat and the type of beard that tells me he knows his shellfish, and who owns *Sylvia May*, a wooden Leigh cockler which he keeps on a fore-and-aft mooring in the Gas House Cut, also known as Gasworks Creek, just opposite. She was carvel-built in 1948 and has been converted for rod and line angling parties by the addition of a wheel house and an open cockpit. Even with these later adaptations her bawley-type lines are unmistakable. Mick takes her down as far as Margate on a tide for a day's fishing. Further west the creek was once lined with houseboats which sat snugly in salting rills, but the whole area was cleared on health grounds in the 1950s. Beyond lies Leigh Marina.

A common trait for boats kept at Leigh was to suffer more wear on the starboard side. This was due to the fore-and-aft mooring in the creek and the boats pointing eastward, downstream, absorbing not only the full force of the sun's rays but the predominant south-westerly winds, always on the same side.

The modern Leigh cockle boats are built of steel and use a suction system in a preferred depth of eight to ten feet, but they can work in depths up to twenty feet. A good cockler doesn't just turn in circles boring a hole in the sand but uses the tide by working up and down an area from deeper water, moving in over shallower ground as the levels rise and working back as the tide turns again. The size of cockle landed is regulated by 16mm gaps in the dredge which allow smaller individuals to fall back. This year each boat was allowed

to land twelve 1-ton bags, or 13.6 cubic metres—which in old measure equates to 500 baskets at six gallons per basket—three times per week; a good yield can be measured by a gallon of meat to every six gallons of shell. The heavy work on the quay is now taken care of by tractors and diggers, and once the shells are placed in the giant pan outside, a conveyer belt system takes over the whole process of cooking and shelling. Gone is the ancient practice of gathering by hand with a rake, and unloading the boat down a narrow plank on foot using a yoke across the fishermen's shoulders with a basket swinging from each side. Today there are nine cockle boats working out of Leigh Creek and five boats that work out of Kent. The fishery is controlled by the Kent and Essex Sea Fisheries Committee. Cockling was done all year round in the early days but the season is now a very short one, 2012 being from mid-June until October, and yields vary from year to year; even so, everywhere about glistens with the golden white of cockle shell grit—'shram' as it is called locally—trodden for decades into every crevice and crack, and covering Cockleshed Beach with a coral-like carpet, giving Leigh Creek its own unique charm.

← *Mick on his Leigh cockler* Sylvia May

5

The River Roach

YIELDING TO THE SEAWARD PULL of *Shoal Waters'* bowsprit, I headed out of the Blackwater, turning south-east to admire the unobstructed view that reaches far across the North Sea.

How many of us must enjoy the trance-like state that open sea sailing can put us in, as repeated waves move the boat up and down and from side to side in an endless soothing motion. Every once in a while a splash of spray comes over the coach-roof soaking one side of us, as if acknowledging our joy and contentment but simultaneously reminding us that although we hold the tiller, nature has a hold on our destiny.

Freshly invigorated by the open seascape, I slid through the Ray Sand Channel swatchway, and passed the Ray buoy to enter the River Crouch for the second time this year. New navigation buoys stood out like brightly coloured lollipops beside the setting sun, creating a blinding picture of a warm summer's evening, slowly fading into the west and directly ahead. Regulars to the river will know there is not much in the way of life as we know it along this stretch of lower Crouch, so when the lonely little pear tree that sits on the skirt of this flatland of plains and marsh comes into view, you can't help but feel sorry for it. To the north, the strange and almost pyramid-like pill box added to the landlocked isolation I was beginning to feel. I was not alone for long, as out of nowhere two magnificent power-

In Narrow Cuts, Havengore Island to port

In the putty at Beagle Dock, Paglesham

boats, as tall as a London bus, muscled past. On the Thames Estuary macho scale my little pocket cutter *Shoal Waters* must be the aqua version of a 2 CV Dolly, and I would not have it any other way.

Their wash was in fact a help and pushed us in the direction I had wanted to go, into the River Roach and the beginning of what was to be some of the most enjoyable creek sailing so far this year. I had a fair tide under, sailing close-hauled, precise and seaman-like, into the oncoming southerly wind. How well I had come to know *Shoal Waters* and her little ways. Each tack called for incremental adjustments to her four sheets that trim her two small headsails, taking full and wide boards, using every inch of the Roach to methodically make our way. We soon passed a few boats anchored by The Quay, at Foulness Island, a very special island where wading birds congregate behind ebbing tides. This island is bounded by a series of creeks and rivers that spread inland to encircle and isolate it from its four smaller neighbours and from the mainland. Havengore and Narrow Cuts creeks bound it to the south-west, the River Roach to the west, and the River Crouch to the north, with the Thames Estuary to the south and east.

It wasn't until the 1920s that the island got its first bridge spanning Havengore Creek. Before this, access was limited to the Broomway, an ancient tidal road that crossed the fabled Maplin Sands to reach the headlands along the island's eastern shore. Visitors could also reach the island by boat, landing at one of the quays in the Rivers Roach and Crouch, or in Shelford Creek. During this time the Thames sailing barge was also a vital link for islanders taking supplies to and from the island.

Due to this relative isolation Foulness has had few inhabitants, but during the 15th century the handful of shepherds and fishermen who chose to live here worked land and sea in harmony. Eel-fishing and wildfowling also became everyday activities on the island, and while elsewhere on our coast ancient fish traps, or 'kettles' as they were also known, date back to Saxon times, this form of kettle fishing was still in use by Foulness fishermen during the early 20th Century. These traps were built not too far from the shore, on the mudflats. Rows of stakes were driven in forming a V shape and covered by netting so that on the retreating tide fish species such as flounders, dabs and sole would be trapped. A line of stakes were also driven in to show a safe passage across the mud back to the shore. At low tide the trapped fish would be recovered by hand by the kettle owners. Wool and dairy farming was also an important industry on the island and it is known that sheep grazed the marshlands for centuries.

Word spread of the island's fertile soil and by 1871 the population had risen to 754 people living in 127 houses. Today there are less than 200 people living there. Another important aspect of island life was the village church. St Mary's Church has suffered from subsidence and has had to be abandoned as its steeple now leans dangerously to one side. Sadly the church closed its doors for the last time in June 2010.

Foulness was known for its two pubs, now long closed. Another inn operated for the duration of the Napoleonic wars. The notable wooden-clad two-storey *George and Dragon* closed in 2007 and was a regular stop for visiting mariners who, after mooring at the quay in the River Roach would ring ahead for the landlord to open up. How's that for service?

The *George* was built in the 17th century but it was during the early 19th century that one of its more memorable licensees kept order in the house. As well as pulling pints he was a revered bare knuckle pugilist who would take on many of his opponents, one of them described as a 'marsh waller', in the garden in front of the pub.

The island's only school closed in 1988 due to lack of pupils, but the building was reopened as the Foulness Heritage Centre in 2003.

Foulness is currently owned by the Ministry of Defence and forms part of the Shoeburyness Artillery Range. Public access to its empty roads is restricted, and the many peculiar structures which lay behind its high sea walls and fences convey mystery and intrigue to those who pass its shores.

I was soon turning at Smallgains Point and Devils Reach, where again I was heading into a blistering sunset. Here the sheets were eased for a gentle reach. Standing at the helm I scandalized the peak of *Shoal Waters*' gaff to a sudden gust that came howling over the rooftop of a building which stood alone on that flat terrain of reclaimed salt water marsh. The landscape remained bleak; a contemporary art form, augmented by a scattering of lonely little signs, painted danger red, emblazoned with warnings and erected along empty sea walls where the footsteps of man rarely tread.

This is a land of the farm field, of cows, pasture and meadow, seals and sea birds. An isolated land far outside the experience of the urban dweller. It was eight or nine years since I last came to this archipelago of islands and creeks under sail, so this was a visit long overdue and gave me the feeling of excitement as if exploring new ground. The small sea-port of Paglesham lay just ahead, a place steeped in history: The remains of Darwin's ship HMS *Beagle* are thought to rest 20 feet beneath the mud at Beagle Dock, and there is the oyster; a resurgence of oyster fishing has once again brought a certain magic to these creeks. Bizarre tales hang in the mists of many of them—during the 1950s a tropical swordfish was caught here.

I could sail on up and drop 'Cold Nose the hook' to seek a seaman's beverage over the bar top of the *Plough & Sail*, that classic

Essex country inn, once a haven of the oyster fisher... a difficult call to make, but made easier by the milk-crate I had below, filled with canned refreshment, and by the croaking call of a friendly seal in the water beside me.

I soon took another turn to port, into Yokesfleet Creek, an even smaller waterway where the wind insisted on following the bow for a heavenly beat down its length. A solitary yacht lay floating at anchor half-way down, the couple aboard enjoying the ambience of the creek on this classic summer evening. I waved as *Shoal Waters* glided gently by and we spoke in passing, sharing a magical moment. The time was now 1830 with high water expected at 2100.

That evening conditions could not be better, a magical recipe of light winds, blue and red skies draped with interesting cloud forms, and warm temperatures. Basically I was taking what I could get by sailing on and on and on, through flat calm creeks with surfaces rippled by swimming seals whose puppy dog faces appeared merrily all around the boat, their calling ringing out over the whole length of the creek, a call not unlike that of a young teenage son who awakes one morning to suddenly speak haplessly in the husky tones of a grown man. Yokesfleet Creek is what I class as one of the 'glorious creeks' that have that extra special piece of magic! But don't tell anyone else.

Shoal Waters was now completely bounded by islands. To port lay uninhabited New England and Havengore Islands, and the wide mass of Foulness with its empty and barren landscape, inhabited by so few; not only by military goings on, but masses of the white seagulls which also flanked the entrance to New England and Shelford Creeks. Both of these creeks have been shut off by the building of the road onto Foulness, but at one time exited into the Thames Estuary. Before the building of this road the only way onto the is-

land was by boat or across the Broomway. To starboard was Potton Island, another flat and barren land commanded by the military but inhabited by grazing cows. The sounds of wildlife were everywhere, and at times I was not quite sure whether it was the seals who were calling or the cows. To think this Spartan paradise was once ear-marked to store government nuclear waste, a shuddering thought.

This whole area is under constant threat from damaging floods that in 1953 caused havoc and destruction. The beguiling sea walls that hide this enchanted wilderness are in constant need of repair and a Potton Island farmer has come up with an ingenious idea which involves the use of helicopters, which are able to move heavy loads of rock quickly, accurately and probably more importantly to-day cheaply, to any newly appearing breach.

In our wake sat Wallasea Island's Baltic Wharf, where ships still visit from the deep water of the Crouch; a busy wharf, haunted by nearby aged and forgotten Lion Wharf at the head of the salty little Lion Creek.

I passed through the Middleway where a stray dinghy lay aban-doned high on the salting fringe of Potton Island; ahead was Rush-ley Island which I almost speared with the bowsprit while my gaze fixed upon its nothingness, before taking another turn to port and into Narrow Cuts, a creek that does what its name implies. Still beating on very short and challenging tacks I was barely maintaining any 'way'. A port marker sits at a metal staircase on the sea wall in Cuts and I was punished for not keeping close enough to it. Franti-cally dancing about on the bow I began jabbing the quanting pole to free *Shoal Waters* from the mud. It being so close to high water I would never get out of here if I became stuck fast. This is a scenario often played out in the silence of a lonely creek and one that *Shoal Waters*, with her heavy load of cruising gear down below, does not take to as freely as did my previous boat, the nimbler little *Huffler*. But stubbornly she just moved into freer mud, but not before I had been hit by the clonking hardness of her boom amidst the kerfuffle.

Warmed around the collar by the sudden activity, I was able to relax a little. I wondered at the bank of the creek along Havengore Island which was to port, a very harsh and seemingly inconsiderate concrete tiled affair. The creek has withies that are placed at many points along its stick-thin length, but unless you are familiar with them you take your pick as to what they signify. I have improved somewhat over the years at playing this guessing game with the withies, so took the challenge of this wonderful little creek with relish. There were further moments of sudden activity as we slowly passed through. I now had sight of Havengore Bridge with its rows of lights which, viewed from the angle I was at, looked like a spaceship from another world. From the sanctuary of Havengore Creek the hum of the massive Thames Estuary just beyond the bridge could be felt; goosebumps and hairs were suddenly raised—a fantastic feeling.

Now in Havengore Creek *Shoal Waters* began dancing in the night breeze where just across the creek, ahead of us, was an old brickworks where fleets of barges once came alongside. The light was disappearing quickly and the tide had just turned, but the wind still blew. I was planning a ceremonial pass through the bridge to anchor for the night on the sands and return to the Blackwater by the open sea route, but was put off by the earlier 1910 weather broadcast of F5-7 later, and instead anchored back up at Shellford Creek, a haven for wild seals in the very thick of the islands and creeks.

6

A Night Passage

A S THE TIDE CAME UP the River Blackwater its timely flow of
bubble and spume began trickling into Goldhanger Creek and
swirling around my *Shoal Waters*. I eagerly waded across squelching
mud to greet her, for I was about to get under way again. I had by
now become familiar with the little gaff cutter and her ways and was
experiencing sailing as of old, single-handedly cruising in a small
boat around the gutways and shoals of the Thames Estuary under
power of sail alone.

Just a couple of months earlier I had adjusted to a slightly different mind-set, where instead of being one step ahead I was now
thinking two or three. Charles Stock liked to use the phrase 'low
animal cunning' to describe what is needed to cruise successfully in
an engineless yacht, and I was amazed at how quickly I had adopted some of these attributes; but I also felt like a boxer in a ring as I
bobbed and weaved at the conditions dealt to me.

A stiff nor-easter was like an overhand right that I ducked and
yielded to, going with its flow. I did so when a break in the weather
allowed the 33NM mile passage up the inshore coast to explore the
forgotten wharf in Johnny All Alone Creek. And on leaving a day
later I dodged ships in the River Stour and Harwich Harbour while
heading out and scraping over the Deben Bar, where on grounding
I had to hop overboard in waders to push us off before we could get

up to Woodbridge. I left on the next tide and went boldly offshore to round the Cork Sand and then scarpered back down the coast on a glorious run past Walton and Clacton. I was feeling on top of the world and began thinking how widely *Shoal Waters* had again spread her wings around her cruising ground.

I crossed the Colne Bar and could just see the mouth of the Blackwater opening up ahead, when with half hour to go before high tide mother nature swung a below-the-belt blow and the north-westerly was cancelled out by the sea-breeze coming from the south-east. Maybe if I hadn't gone round the Cork I would have been safely inside the Blackwater by now and would have anchored by the Mersea shore as planned to await the following tide upriver? The next hour sat in the doldrums felt as desperate as a set of fingernails scraping on a chalkboard. High tide came and went. I began a hopeless drift further out to sea. I passed the North-West Knoll going the wrong way. I was in deep water in more ways than one and then the flashbacks began, of sweetly popping two strokes coming to the rescue— if only...

In all truth these were the exact type of situations I wanted to face alone. This was my chain of thought at the time as perhaps only then would I emerge from the sea's forge a diversified sailor. I remained calm and was about to sling the hook over, when after what seemed like hours the north-westerly came back in with a vengeance and all hell broke loose, as sails flogged wildly until I gripped the sheets, reining them in until rigid, and *Shoal Waters* shot off like a cruise missile. My heart raced as thrillingly I blazed over the ebb into the Blackwater in a 10NM mile trail along the slack margins, and into the shallower northern route into Thirslet Creek, in a record time of three and a half hours, when I could go no further and stuck fast in mud teasingly in the lower end of my home creek. Alas I completed the trip by coming in on the evening's tide around midnight.

I was again at the mercy of the winds and would be governed by the tide as I left my shoal-studded, creek-infested haven that is the River Blackwater to head south for a 25NM journey to the River Crouch, a deep cut of water that penetrates far inland but, unlike the Blackwater, has few creeks. Already the evenings had begun drawing in, which meant we would be sailing after dark, roughly in two hours' time. I unhooked *Shoal Waters'* cockpit cover to shuffle aboard and slip out of the mud boots, hanging them from her stern cleat. I raised the main and backed the staysail to weather, climbed forward and let go of the mooring line.

She wasn't having any of it, and remained stuck fast until a more forceful westerly came in, jarring her into life, and suddenly she surged into free water. We were off, set loose and toddling our way out of the creek. The sun fell away to the west over the lonely marshes a while later as we reached toward Osea Island. Half the sky was now black with stars, appearing as I ran her into a calm bay in the lee of the island, about 15ft offshore, and dropped the anchor. The coming night would be long, so I set about making dinner.

I washed the meal down with a couple of mugs of strong tea. The caffeine would keep me alert, I hoped, as I scrambled about the deck in complete darkness, one hand holding part of the boat and one feeling for the chain to raise the hook. As I did so, she moved with the tide: her bow slowly came around to point downriver, and with her beam on the wind she sailed herself just long enough for me to move aft and step back down into the cockpit. I noted in the log the time was 2115.

On my port side the ruined pier's two green lights shone brightly now, and faint tungsten lights hung in the darkness beyond. These were windows on the façade of Osea Island's Edwardian-style manor house, originally built by a brewer as a sanctuary for recovering alcoholics.

I'd switched the navigation lights on before weighing anchor so we were visible, and I picked out the red light of the Marconi buoy as it flashed in groups of two to the east of us. Within minutes we had passed it and began heading toward the green light of the Thirslet that marks a huge spit in mid-river and to the north. As it was so dark I couldn't make out any boats along the deep water moorings to the south: this had me riding a little too close for comfort down to Stone.

As soon as I got a visual on anything resembling a boat I put in a tack and headed north for the dark abyss of open water, for I needed as much sea as possible to make any way eastward, downriver, and pass Thirslet, where the deep channel broadens to just under a mile wide. This would allow me to free off a little and use the current to rush straight ahead for the fixed red on the man-made concrete island of the Baffle, two miles further east.

I find it is around this point when 'easting' out of the River Blackwater, alone and not using a chart plotter or GPS, that obtaining a definite fix tends to become a little more interesting. Lights that are seen out to sea blend in with those within the river, such as the white navigation lights of the Nass Beacon which leads you into Mersea Quarters, Bradwell's tide pole, and red lights on the Baffle — even house lights on the shoreline.

As I safely passed between them I remained confused by the string of red lights out to sea and the stream of pearl-white lights that glared from Mersea Island. These resembled a fishing boat with deck lights, but this time the lights just didn't change as I got, as I thought, closer and left them to port. I leant forward and squinted to read the numbers on the compass dial, which showed we were heading 108°, east-southeast.

The time was now 2355, and slowly things began to unfold. I could make out the green light of the Bench Head and Colne Bar over the port bow, and the white lights I had thought were a fishing boat became the town of Brightlingsea, about five miles away. The string of reds parted into two groups even further and out to sea, one to the south and one ahead that reached northwards. They were the lights of the London Array and Gunfleet wind farms that to me resembled London's Regent Street decoratively lit up for Christmas. A gift if heading up the Wallet or down Swin, but next to useless where I was heading as I was three miles offshore and, as passage planning goes, way past the point of no return.

It was time I turned south into the Ray Sand Channel. By now I was also a good mile to seaward past the danger of the unlit cardinal beacons that point out two wrecks on the Dengie mudflats, and began a glorious plough through faintly-lit waves that shimmered under a half-lit moon.

A fair wind now came from aft—a Force 4 over the port quarter. As I pulled the staysail in on its Wykeham-Martin furler and let the mainsail sheet run out, a calm and quietness surrounded us. I could hear a pin drop and every creak in the boat echoed. I took a back bearing off the Bench Head light while I had the chance but it was hopeless trying to keep to it: even so, all was good in the world for a while as we sailed on down channel.

But we would soon meet the ebb head-on as it left the River Crouch, which was just over seven nautical miles further south from our position, flushing through the Ray Sand swatchway in a north-easterly direction. Soon a choppy sea had risen and the odd lash of salt came over the bow. I could hear the classic tunes which softly played from the radio in the cabin; this warmed my heart and allowed me to delight in the excitement of the night's cruising. I began sounding with the cane to find an average of 6ft on the starboard side, which was quite normal for where we now were this far down the channel.

How I wished I'd eaten that tin of carrots with dinner earlier though, for with eyes wide open I searched for the new Safe Water buoy in complete darkness. From my dead reckoning I sensed we were now near the buoy, and as it too is unlit I feared it would smash the boat to pieces if we collided head-on at our pace of four knots.

I had quite fresh memories of a similar situation, albeit in a different vessel, and moving considerably quicker, when four of us took the 90-year-old Thames barge Phoenician round to Southend just weeks earlier. We had motored through the Wallet Spitway into the East Swin and on into the darkness of night, passing the Whitaker and Maplin, the West Swin and South West Barrow buoys. Between us we knew the way by eye, ear and feel but sailed blind into The Warp, where one of us felt it best to go below and switch on the barge's chartplotter to double check our navigation, for we were searching in vain for a visual on the Blacktail Spit buoy which should have been flashing green in groups of three every ten seconds. It was unlit due to a broken light but we did eventually find it as two of us kept watch by sitting on the anchor windlass, calling aloud to the helm with a sigh of relief as its deathly silhouette stormed past around midnight on our port side, just feet from us, when it should have been to starboard...

Suddenly a huge dark shadow shot past on my port side. I sighed in relief for it was the marker, and I also now had a definite fix. I checked the compass again to make sure we were on course heading south-west, and would be clear of the Buxey Sand, a six-mile-long sandbank just to the east, which in fact is marked by the fabled though also unlit Buxey Beacon.

I steered us a couple of degrees west to allow for the set of tide, and made a note of the time in that kind of unreadable shorthand scribble you do while under way. The water soon began to shoal and the centreplate made contact with the sands beneath. I hauled it up and, guided by my trusty pea stick, funnelled into the bottleneck of the swatchway where I dropped the anchor to wait for the tide to turn. It was 0145.

Standing on the bow while setting the anchor in 3ft of water felt what I imagined balancing a surfboard on top of a tightrope in outer space would be like. I was miles from civilisation on a shallow sea that was choppy as hell-on-high-water, only this was near low water: the sea's surface now glittered from the reflection of golf-ball-sized stars and a crescent moon that suddenly shone brightly. Nevertheless, when I climbed inside the cabin I pointed the torch at the barometer to see the needle still held fast to the happy side of the dial which added to a promise of clear blue skies for the following day.

Patiently I lay in wait, or more accurately got thrown about wildly for a few hours by an enraged sea that rushed powerfully across the sands, before setting off again two hours into the favour of a new flood and breaking dawn. I was now heading inland again, away from the open sea and the swatchways. I held the tiller as *Shoal Waters* pitched, splashing her way west, skirting the steep-to banks of Foulness Sands, past colourful starboard and port-hand channel buoys, when a thought came to me—she knows the swatchways better than I ever will.

7

Mystery in Lion Creek

I TOOK A DEEP BREATH and my shoulders fell as I exhaled. I had cleared the last of the swinging moorings while passing through Burnham on Crouch and was able to free off a little. As I did so 500 deep water moorings at Essex Marina passed close-by to port, while Burnham Yacht Harbour, home to two RNLI boats, was opposite. Just a few more moorings in mid-river to pass and I was deep inland again, at Baltic Wharf, where ships still call regularly from northern Europe to deliver steel or timber. Just west of the wharf is an insignificant-looking opening in the marsh; enter it and you are in Lion Creek, a whole micro-world on its own, and one I had come here to explore. Across the river was neighbouring Creeksea, on the north shore, the place looking as pretty now as it has done for centuries, with its old brick cottages and Tudor buildings leading down to the water, and the sailing club slipway originally built in World War II to service RAF rescue boats. Not much else appears to have changed in this little area of the Crouch that manages to retain a timeless feel.

It is said that during the 17th century Lord Mildmay, who was Keeper of the Crown Jewels under Charles I and who owned Creeksea Place, a wonderful Tudor building just up on the hill, was taken from here to the Tower of London for, with eleven other state elders, signing the King's death warrant, though it is also said he was later pardoned by Charles II.

Entering Lion Creek

Lion Creek near low water

I sailed around the Creeksea Sailing Club moorings before looking back across the river and lining up a transit route into Lion Creek's approximately 100 feet wide mouth, which was now facing opposite and right beside Baltic Wharf on Wallasea Island. The creek is deeply cut with a good 15 feet of water in the gut if coming in on a high tide, and it has steep-shelving mud slopes that are marked 2.7 metres above chart datum on my Admiralty chart, that can trap the unwary skipper, and are topped with the green glory that is East Coast saltmarsh. This marsh abuts an encasing six-foot-high grassy sea wall creating a creek haven that is a joy to sail in and one that slowly narrows the deeper you enter, but with this westerly wind persisting I ambled into the waterway on a beam reach, playfully probing the margins as we went, penetrating inward until out of sight of the Crouch, and where I had to "ready about" a few times to round a westward bend that camouflaged a massively humped mud shoal that tried to claim us.

The banks of the creek were coming together now, embracing us fully. It was time to fold *Shoal Waters*' little russet brown wings and gently paddle the rest of the way up. The last few yards took us into a tight cut at Lion Wharf, where just a few jabs with the quant pole positioned her; I anchored in five feet of water at 0843 to cook steamed kippers for breakfast, right beside a solitary wooden hut that is thought to be an old oyster shed. This is quite possible as the creek, like many others in this area in the 19th century, was used for highly profitable oyster farming, and is profusely indented with hand-dug oyster pits along its saltmarsh banks.

The wharf at the creek's head once had the traffic of many Thames spritsail barges during the heyday of working sail. Quite unique to Lion Creek today are the mysterious solid wooden blocks, of which I counted 30, scattered all about on the top of the saltings or part-buried in muddy rills off the main creek. Maybe they had broken free from a tether of connecting chains during some gale-blown night. Each block is approximately ten feet long by six feet wide and four feet deep and on closer inspection has four steel air-tight drums encased within and held together by giant iron rods with large mooring rings. Their history is worthy of note as they were some of thousands made for floating defence booms that spanned the mouth of the River Thames from Shoeburyness in Essex to Minster in Kent, and other East Coast rivers, to thwart enemy in-cursion during WWII. Huge nets were hung from them to trap sub-marines and some of the blocks had spikes on top to prevent ships going over the boom. They were sold off after the war and used as pontoons and now resemble giant planters, especially those that have become overgrown with saltmarsh. However they ended up here, these wooden blocks and many other man-made objects, such as wrecks or old docks, that I come across lend a distinct charm to the forgotten and lonely backwaters I explore.

Knowing where to anchor in a creek when you come in at high water can be a hazardous business, so if I have not done a scout-ing visit on foot I always sound forward and aft for level ground, and sweep the cane underneath the boat both sides as the water level drops to check for any protruding stumps that could hole her. Where I had anchored for the night the bottom was flat and just per-fect for drying out, and once the tide had left the creek it became the feasting-ground for curlews and terns; I climbed ashore to find wild mushrooms as big as jam-jar lids growing along the rim of the saltings.

Lion Creek was once named Canewdon Creek for it is sited in Canewdon Parish, at the foot of a belt of green land that rises west-ward to a steep hillside behind which the evening sun sets. There

About to wade out to join *Shoal Waters*

Night Passage

Bow Locks

Havengore Bridge

Lion Wharf, Lion Creek

Shoal Waters snug in Gunner's Creek, St Peter-on-the-Wall in the background

The author and Dave in Goldhanger Creek

Red Sands Towers, a World War II anti-aircraft structure

Beaumont Quay, built from stones of the old London Bridge replaced in 1831
The hulk of barge *Rose* in Beaumont Cut

St Andrew's Church and Mission, at 'Bawley Bay', Gravesend

On the Bawley *Marigold*

Remains of ancient fish traps at Collins Creek on the Blackwater

London Stone, near the mouth of Yantlet Creek

Martello Tower at Jaywick

Exploring Yantlet Creek in my duck punt *Winkler*

Canewdon village is found with its ancient church from whose tower are some of the most far-reaching views across the Crouch valley and greater Essex. Canewdon is a name which you could be forgiven for thinking was derived from that great Dane, King Canute, who it is said came to this part of the coast in 1016, after his failed siege of London, to battle with the King of England, Edmund II, and triumph in the valley between Canewdon and Ashingdon hill. But it is thought to have derived from much earlier Saxon meanings such as 'don' which meant a hill settlement.

The creek ends at Lion Wharf beside Creeksea Ferry Road that connects the mainland to Wallasea Island and also blocks another cut to the east that would have joined Paglesham Creek, encircling the Island. There is also a dam across the main body of the creek to the west in the form of the sea wall, beyond which the creek has become a freshwater inland pool named Lion Creek Nature Reserve, a Site of Special Scientific Interest. Old maps show the creek would have originally made its way westward through marshland where King Canute is thought to have made camp, before it enters the River Crouch again near South Fambridge.

Lion Creek is best explored a couple of hours around high water when it's possible to get ashore. I eventually left at high water that same evening for the 25NM journey back to my mooring, where I arrived safely the following day. Trip tally 50NM with an average of 2.5kts made good under wind and tide alone.

The Wild Sea Coast

I CALL THE STRETCH OF COASTLINE *that reaches from Shoeburyness in the south to Bradwell-juxta-Mare in the north The Wild Sea Coast. Very few people inhabit it, hardly any public roads reach the sea walls, and very few buildings spoil its wide open spaces. Wild plants thrive here, rabbits, foxes and deer roam freely and adders swarm undisturbed in marsh and arable land which extends for miles. The shallowness of the sea and the short tidal window make it difficult to explore in a sailing boat. However I have managed to explore every creek that pierces it in Shoal Waters, and have rambled its length many times on foot.*

If the tide is flooding it's an easy matter to pull into a small inlet such as Howe Creek, an outfall where on a spring ebb the waters rush out so fast that it is nigh on impossible to control a small boat as you are tossed across its turbulent exit from the Dengie Flats. But inside all is tranquil and after a hop across samphire-adorned ditches I can walk beside the soft, plump, salt-white leaves of sea purslane and run my hands through the long damp grass in the still air of dawn.

Every so often an onshore easterly brings with it an eerie sea-mist that enrobes everything in sight. How strange it is to be lost in a magnificent 'sea-garden' of ragwort, sea-weed and aster for a few fleeting moments, to be invigorated as everything around flowers in full glory as soon as the sun beats its way through again.

Walk this coast and you will come across a variety of reeds. Reed was once gathered along inland and coastal marshes and used for mattresses; here it spouts from dykes and ditches below the sea walls that were built to reclaim these remote marshland prairies. With their thick, tall stalks with tops resembling long brown cigars, reeds wave about wildly, and add enormously to the draw of the place.

No two days are the same along this breezy coast, the only constant being the ebb and flow of the tides that bring a gourmet feast for the wild birds. To set a small sail and cruise into this 'sea-country' is joy indeed—as it is to pick a handful of winkles, mussels or oysters along the muddy tide-lines for a true taste of the sea.

8

A Remote Promontory

HEAD EAST MY FRIEND, over there, down that lane—yes
that's the one. Go through the gate and keep going until you
reach the end. You'll be alright. "Thank you kindly sir". That's ok,
you enjoy your walk—and mind those pebble stones, I said, adjusting my shoulder bag and shuffling toward the lane myself. This was
no ordinary lane though as this unassuming little farm track is part
of a two-mile stretch of Roman road that cuts through the centre
of a promontory that juts out toward the North Sea. To the north
of this chunk of land is the River Blackwater and to the south, the
River Crouch. These two rivers frame and isolate one of the most
remote areas in all of England's East Coast, the Dengie Peninsula, a
quiet corner in the county of Essex, which makes up the greater part
of the Dengie Hundred[1].

The track has felt the footsteps of Roman soldiers for it was
built around AD42 when the legions first came to Britain. It runs
in a straight line almost east to west from the site of a former sea

---

1   The Hundreds were the old land divisions inside Essex and are thought to
have come from the very beginnings of the county when measures of land were
given out to Saxon warrior lords. There were 19 hundreds, five of them half-
hundreds, in total with names such as Rochford, Tendring and Chelmsford.
One theory is that each division would have been deemed suitable to support a
hundred families.

fort called Othona, which is one of nine that were placed strategically around the coast to guard the remote outposts of the Roman Empire against marauding barbarian tribes such as the Angles, the Jutes and their most feared of all, the Saxons.

Half of the fort has been lost to the sea but it is highly likely that Roman merchant ships, as well as gilded Roman galleys, full with armour-clad warriors, would have regularly pulled alongside. Coins from the reign of 24 different Emperors who ruled over Britain during a period of 400 years have been discovered at the site, and tell us just how vitally important this lonely promontory outpost once was. Digging at the site is forbidden as it now comes under the legal protection of a Scheduled Monument, but every once in a while burrowing rabbits throw up a piece of Roman earthenware that has lain undisturbed for up to 2,000 years.

The main fort could well have been built in AD286 as this was when the military commander of the Roman Empire, Carausius, sent Maximian to Britain in a concerted effort to put a stop to the troublesome Saxons. But it would be three and a half centuries later, when the Romans had long since fled Britain, that Christian Bishop St Cedd would make his way down the east coast from Lindisfarne. He landed on the south shore of the River Blackwater, which was then known as The Pant, in 653 and soon went about building the small chapel of St Peter-on-the-Wall from the stone ruins that lay all around the former fort, in what was by now the land of the East Saxons, later to become known as Essex. Other marauders were to follow such as the Danes who came across the North Sea in their long-ships to plunder our coastline. They would have been drawn to the solitary cathedral overlooking the sea, like a swarm of hornets.

For many people who pass the chapel today, whether by land or sea, its sheer presence is enough to invoke a feeling of solitude, but to step inside is to be spell-bound. A deep calm and quiet fills the almost empty space where on cold stone floors sparse oak benches sit sheltered by the stone walls of this typically simple Saxon building, muting whispering echoes of those raiding Vikings hell bent on gathering Danegeld, which was a type of monetary payment frequently made by the Saxons after the battle of Maldon in 991 in order to be left in peace.

What is known of the chapel's history is interesting enough but it is remarkable that the building still stands, helped no doubt that in 1066 and after the Norman Conquest, William I became King of England and the chapel came under ownership of Benedictine monks, who it is said took good care of it for over 300 years. A little later, in 1442, the chapel is noted as having a small tower with two bells in it, but hardly anything is known of its history in the following centuries other than it coming under the ownership of various Bishops, Abbots, lords of the manor and land owners. Late in the 18th century a sketch showed that the chapel again had a tower which in Tudor times was used as a lighthouse or beacon. By 1774 it was marked on a map in the British Museum as being a barn, and subsequently went on to become a cattle shed where the animals would roam in and out through gaping holes in its walls. Smugglers are reputed to have stored contraband there. Finally ownership of the chapel was transferred from estate owner Mr C W Parker, who also owned a fleet of spritsail barges that were based in nearby Bradwell Creek, to a group of trustees who undertook the restoration of the building, and on 22 June 1920 the ancient shrine was re-dedicated to worship.

Built on the lip of the former Roman fort is a small two-roomed, blackened weatherboard cottage. It is tucked away behind a thick wooded area to the south which gives the hut shelter but also means

Linnett's Cottage

it can be easily passed unnoticed by walkers. The cottage closely resembles the Signal Cottage on Foulness Island, about twelve miles
south from here. This is no coincidence as they were both built to
house signal officers in the Napoleonic wars and formed part of a
line of semaphore signalling stations that enabled the Admiralty in
London to send and receive messages along this low coast within
minutes rather that by conventional means of a horse that would
take many hours. The front of the cottage faces east where there is a
tiny garden on the fringe of the saltings, facing the bleakness of the
sea.

I often come to this little area in my small boat, finding my way
in through 'Gunners Creek' and the network of small rills that fill
to the very foot of the little cottage garden. It is a place of solitude
where wild birds over-winter in large numbers. One man lived alone
here back in the 50s and generations of his family before him. His
name was Walter Linnett and he was a master of the old ways of
fishing, fowling and hunting. It was not uncommon for city gen-
try to come to his small home to learn from him the secrets of the
marsh, as he had truly learnt how to survive in what is to many an
inhospitable place. After Linnett finally left his home bird watchers moved in and used it as their base for observing the varied and
often rare species that come to this shore. As the birdwatchers grew
in number, a new, much larger hut was erected just to the side of
the cottage. Today birdwatchers no longer stay in Linnett's Cottage
due to modern health and safety issues, but I was able to spend time
inside and gain an insight into what it would have been like to live
in this remote corner of England. On entering the doorway there is
a small kitchen directly in front, a turn left and there are two door-
ways; left again into the lounge or right into the bedroom. There are
two smaller ledged boarded doors (one off each room) which access

the rear lean-to. The two main rooms measure approximately ten feet square and have a Georgian style sash window in each with a central brick built fireplace and chimney. The lounge room walls are wooden boards of nine inches width with bead-butt detail and are a rose-red in colour, a tone that naturally occurs with aged timber, and are finished in a clear sheen varnish. Two gas pendant lights are fixed either side of the window which is indication enough that this tiny cottage is not connected to the national grid. Legend has it that it was this window that a ghost with no legs was seen to come straight through and enter the room during the night. From my experiences during the many nights I have spent out on the nearby marsh creeks camping on board my small boat, I have never once witnessed the presence of a ghost, but I have felt the roar of the tide and the lashing of its salt spume that can be thrown about wildly during an easterly gale. Outside the cottage would have laid a scattering of gun punts and hunting nets, eel spears and other associated paraphernalia used in the old ways of gathering food for one's supper.

To the north of the fort and also unseen from the sea wall, crouching low behind bushes and dense trees, can be found a more recent settlement called The Othona Community, founded by former RAF Chaplain Norman Motley in 1946. When he first came here he knew he had found a special place that was perfect for his vision of bringing together people of former warring nations to gain a better understanding of each other and for reflection. They originally camped in tents and used a small hut but now have a sustainable purpose-built facility.

The Othona Community today has people come from all walks of life and all faiths to experience living with others in a unique environment. It is run by a small core of workers and volunteers, and

visitors pay a nominal fee to stay here. For those of a material per-
suasion it could be said this is not luxury living, and if you are alone
and choose to stay you may well be sharing a room, but accommoda-
tion is more than adequate. Some people come for a weekend while
others stay for months.

I visited the community by boat on a gloriously sunny day when
the St Peter's mudflats would later bake like brown ovens, and was
warmly welcomed with a mug of tea, and more tea, and then told I
could help myself to even more as and when required. I sat in the
large communal lounge in one of the dozen or so sofas and arm-
chairs. The building is built mostly out of pine and has huge lami-
nated wooden beams spanning the open roof space. I felt at home
immediately and searched my diary for an excuse to stay a full week.
I watched people come and go from the dormitory rooms and kitch-
en area, which are at the other end of the main lounge I was seated
in, and the outside areas. A group gathered in the main garden outside the fully glazed lounge and began singing joyously while others
watched. From my own travels along the marshes of this sea coast
I often experience something spiritual, and when the time came for
me to leave I felt I had not only gained a further insight into this spiritual state of mind but also how positive an effect this place can have
on more than one person at any given time.

Back to the small area of raised land where during hot summers
a riot of colourful meadow plants sway in the breeze before shelv-
ing naturally into the sea-marsh at the foot of Othona. Leaving the
promontory one is on the sea wall again where heading south are
mile after mile of saltmarsh stuffed full with sea purslane and profusely dented with desolate creeks, home to hen harriers, redshank
and curlew. And where the waves break a dusting of golden shell
beaches is home to a thousand screaming gulls. Agricultural plains

as flat as a board spread as far as the eye can see, draining into dykes and ditches which feed outfalls that pierce the sea wall, where rare plants such as yellow-horned poppies grow and chiffchaffs are heard all the way to the deep cut in the land that is the southern boundary of this peninsula—the River Crouch.

9

Old Salts up the Creeks

FRIDAY'S DRIVING RAIN held bleak prospects for any decent sailing on Saturday, but as I climbed over *Shoal Waters'* coaming later that evening racing clouds began to uncover a winking moon. Its light shone over the creek in hopeful flashes until the clouds had dissipated. The last of the tide had slowly ebbed and the boat sat dead still on the mud, only a north-westerly wind irritatingly plucking at the rigging, raising dreadful notes as it went, and sinking them into the Stumble mud where more than fifty geese suddenly took flight. They had been startled by my fumbling attempts to remove my mud boots and I watched as their silhouettes flew across the distant white moon.

Instead of the usual rush down to the boat from work, which seemed to be the pattern of my sailing at the start of the year, how civilised my cruising had become only a few months later. A consistency had set in as I was now getting down to the boat on a Thursday or Friday and leisurely preparing her for sailing. On this occasion I walked back over the mud to fill the water cans at the club before cooking an evening meal on board. After dinner I set the alarm and shuffled into the bunk early with a book to read. The wind still moaned outside as I fell asleep half an hour later.

When I awoke the next morning sun was beaming through the centre porthole. I got dressed lying down and could feel the boat was ready to weigh anchor by her tugging at the mooring buoy. I opened the canvas door and could see she was floating about in just over a foot of water. Then I remembered I was sailing with crew today, as I had a friend and fellow Blackwater small-boat sailor Dave Selby joining me for some creek-crawling along the north shore. Dave and I had made a few attempts this year to go creek-sailing in company, with Dave in his Sailfish 18 *Marlin* and me in *Shoal Waters*, but for one reason or another we hadn't managed it. This time we had arranged to meet at the last minute, at 1000 the next day, and that I would be skipper, over coffee at a deli in Wenlock Way, Maldon.

Saturday morning came and Dave appeared on the sea wall nice and early. I was impressed at his punctuality and watched as he made his way down the slip and across the creek towards me, only to become entangled by the deceptive mud that abounds in Gold-handger Creek. "Don't panic" I yelled, "I'll pull the boat toward you and you can climb aboard then." I let go of the mooring buoy and walked the boat over and Dave was soon on board. The ship's kettle was put to good use immediately, before the reefed mains'l was raised, the jib unfurled 'aback,' and we slowly sailed away from the shore and into deeper water.

Dave had left his trusty mascot, his dog Bart, home alone for our little adventure "He would only have eaten the sausage sandwiches I've made for lunch," he pleaded. Dave had brought the sun out with him though, and a fresh F4 north-westerly which had the boat ploughing through a rising chop as we let some centre plate down and headed toward Bawley Creek, Osea Island.

We were soon sailing around the entrance where we could have a good look at the creek but were still a little early on the tide to get right in, so we hardened up and took off along the shoreline to Shipwreck Beach, and then a push on the tiller pointed us north-

wards, over into Wilkins Creek where we found huge flocks of oys-
tercatchers on the saltings. I went forward and dropped anchor in
four and a half feet, just to steady us for a while so that we could sit
in smooth water and take in the scenery, while Dave went below and
re-appeared through the companionway with another cuppa. This
was a good crew indeed. And rightly so as Dave has sailed across the
Atlantic and knows only too well the benefits of a contented ship.

Then suddenly another small boat appeared—a blue Cornish
Shrimper motored into Wilkins Creek! No, I hadn't had too much
to drink last night and was not seeing things; this was for real—
heading straight towards us. The boat came up close, alongside—
nearly spearing little *Shoal Waters* with his bowsprit in so doing,
were I not there fending her off by hand. The skipper said hello and
no sooner was motoring off again. A friendly bunch of folk they are
in the Blackwater!

We upped the main again and weighed anchor. I took Dave
through Winkle Ditch, which is a sweet little hideout I often lay in,
and which takes you between the saltings and out into the main river
again. Dry out here and you will find this place is a deep-pile carpet
of black shelled winkles.

To explore the area further we had a lively sail over the flood,
eastward, back past Goldhanger Creek, and slipped past the shingle
spit at Joyce's Creek, which for the micro cruiser in certain conditions becomes a mini Cape Horn. The combinations of wind and
tide often throw up local sailing conditions inside the Blackwater
that can be likened to a revered section of blue water ocean. Another
one can be when sailing out of Bradwell Creek and over to Mersea
Island, this can often be the Atlantic crossing of the estuary dinghy
sailor. We were into flat water again where I commented to Dave
"As soon as the tide turns the Stumble will become a mill pond in

minutes." Dave was busy ooh-ing and aah-ing about the beauty of Joyce's and the red-brick Georgian farm house at the head of the creek—I agreed wholeheartedly then felt another cuppa coming on.

We were soon sailing again though. Dave took the helm and guided us out of Joyce's Creek. It was now high water and a few boats had begun moving about around Goldhanger Creek as we sailed into it. *Shoal Waters'* plate came up as we were entering deep into the creek, sailing around the moored boats in a succession of tacks while the sounding cane began working over the starboard side. Dave was enjoying the sail so much that I hoped he had not seen me miss picking up my mooring buoy twice, it's just that these days I like to get the buoy directly beside, at elbows length—just so, while I am still sitting, and when I can clip on and be civilised!

10

The Ton

THE JOURNEYS I HAD MADE SOUTH the previous three weekends must surely have cost poor *Shoal Waters* a solid ¼-inch of steel in the form of a toll grazed from her centerplate, for the continual crossing back and forth over the hard sands of the Ray. But relief did come for her when the wind eventually went round to the south, which allowed me to get up the coast and deep into Suffolk's rolling sea-country where her centreplate fared much better, while being put to good use entering over the narrow but tricky width of the Ore Bar, where on making contact it sang a sound as piercing as the curlew! The following week the wind had gone east and an extended forecast, which I chose to go with, gave northeast followed by south-east. This would be a good opportunity for a cruise down to the Lower Thames. In theory a fair wind in both outward and inward legs of the cruise.

I boarded *Shoal Waters* just before midnight on Thursday in order to be away on the Friday morning's tide. High water would be at 0342. On leaving at 0430 I set the topsail which got us moving and into the deeper water lower down the creek. By 0530 the sky was overcast as we passed Mersea Island, and as is often the case short chop had risen to large swells while heading toward the Wallet Spitway, where I had to pull down a reef and take in the tops'l. Once through the swatchway and into the East Swin we rode the waves to gybe round the South Whitaker. At 0830 I furled the jib and staysail and began to feel my lower back pressing against the cockpit coamings during a gallivanting run under a full mainsail and a fair tide. While underway any chart work, or rather 'Kneecap Navigation,' is done on my lap in the tiny cockpit and it is here that the hand-bearing compass is placed near enough to grab.

Cruising around seven or eight miles offshore no useful landmarks were visible, but there are plenty of sea-marks nearby one can use so I took a three-point fix on those that could be seen around us: Barrow Beacon, Knock John Tower and the Whitaker Beacon; then picked out the navigation buoys ahead through my 7x50 binoculars before they passed in succession as if falling like dominoes—Maplin Edge, Maplin, West Swin, South West Barrow, the mystically named Blacktail Spit, and the two measured mile marks, where the wind died and the Thames Estuary suddenly became a smooth moving carpet of flickering silver, and we began heading west to pass the Shoebury Beacon at 1355.

By 1600 I watched the train on England's longest pier, Southend, taking passengers to the end as I sailed west of it and up the adjacent Leigh Creek to say hello to a couple of friends on Billet Wharf. The delightful 30ft Paglesham-built barge yacht *Nancy Grey* sat tugging at her mooring, and I passed within feet of her when I left to round the pier end again and sail into smooth water and tuck in tight in the lee of a rising easterly wind, where I dropped the anchor in the soft sand of Thorpe Bay at 1840. With the centreplate and rudder hauled up *Shoal Waters* touched bottom just over an hour later at 1945, when I had a walk ashore and sat and watched the sun fall away over Southend—a blissful end to a wonderful day's cruising.

Saturday I got away at 0420 with the aim of getting across the Thames to Kent, which took two hours of focused sailing in light airs to cover 3NM. For a transit I used the 19th century Grain Tower which sat on the Grain Spit across the river due south. This strange tower resembles the Martello Towers, built to repel Napoleon, that are found along the Essex and Suffolk coast, and it once guarded the River Medway entrance. All the while I dodged shipping that seemed to be entering and leaving the Thames every 10 or 15 minutes.

Eventually I joined the full force of the ebbing tide about half a mile west of the Medway No. 1 buoy, and turned east to run with its force, and suddenly was charging along at more than 4 knots. I pointed *Shoal Waters* in toward the Isle of Sheppey where we sailed for a time in shallow water and by 0720 had met the swirling mass of water on the edge of The Cant, where we rattled along the contour for a time in a very confused sea which sucked and pulled us past the East Cant buoy. With a fair wind perhaps we just may have been able to ride the tide all the way down to Margate? However, at 0800 *Shoal Waters*' bowsprit had sniffed out the Red Sands Towers that were, along with a handful of others such as the nearby Shivering Sands Towers and the Knock John and Roughs Tower further north, built to defend the Thames Estuary from enemy aircraft in World War II.

We sailed right round the rusting iron sea fort, which drew my gaze like a magnet, in light airs but at least the wind was being kind as it had now gone east, which would be handy for the return, so I headed south to put the light breeze on the beam and reach until we could see the Kentish seaport of Whitstable through the morning mist. The dip in the landscape beside Whitstable was the mouth of The Swale, which was on my Plan Variables list. We would have en-

Shoal Waters on the sand at Thorpe Bay →

tered to go round Sheppey on the flood if we had more of a working breeze. The temperature began to rise and the four layers of clothing and my woollen hat that I'd been wearing for comfort on the fresh dark mornings could now come off again.

I felt sorry for two Dutch yachts that came past heading out toward the North Sea, so I gave them a big wave as they had obviously been held up by the north-easterlies, but were now making some ground eastward and homeward on the promise of the coming south-easterly. I now had my own problems for as the heat rose the wind fell away. Concerned a little that I may have an enforced stay in the picturesque county referred to as the Garden of England, I set off toward the north-west and by 1020 was heading a course 320M on the steering compass toward South Shoebury. I stood off out to sea in slight hesitation thinking it safer to get back over to Essex when I could see no ships coming from either direction.

By 1150 I had passed west of the South Shoebury buoy for the second time in two days but this time heading a course of 340M toward an artificial island just on the edge of the Maplin Sands. At 1215 I dropped anchor at Maplin Island, a shingle home to sea birds, in 6 feet of water and put the kettle on and prepared lunch while patiently waiting for the sands to cover. For those sailors that use the sea environment to step back a little and relax from hectic or busy work schedules, it may be a shuddering thought to learn that this island was put here in 1973 as a trial during a campaign to build London's third airport right here on the Essex coast. It had huge local opposition and eventually came to nothing but the idea has resurfaced again and today there are reports being drawn up on the suitability of the Thames Estuary, including here on the Maplin Sands, once more for an airport.

At 1330 a couple in a catamaran motored close by and the lady called over "are you waiting to take the short cut through Havengore Bridge?"

"I sure am," I replied. I then added—"in another hour there should be enough water to get over the sands."

"Oh that's good as we have never done it so can we follow you in?"

"Of course you can—that would be my pleasure," I said.

I settled back down below in the bunk and lay looking up through the forward hatch opening. The high-pitched whistling of wind through *Shoal Waters'* rigging was becoming louder and louder and her anchor chain grated noisily as it gripped the Samson post to ever rising swells and the new flood now racing past. At 1420 I hoisted sail and was away again. I sailed around the south side and passed west of the artificial island and steered a compass course of 10 degrees northward. Sounding with my eight feet cane I could not touch the bottom. The afternoon sea breeze had risen dramatically too, enough that I was now embroiled in an arm-wrestling match with the tiller. I could not sail her for she was now over-canvassed for the immediate conditions—I needed to heave to, pull down a reef and furl the jib to settle her down. I reefed down quite comfortably considering gusts of F5 were now lifting the shallow sea over the Maplin Sands. It's deep enough water to become a real danger in a F4/5 though and by 1440 we had reached the beacon that marks a wreck and the point to turn north-east to pick up the line of posts that lead inwards toward the creek.

At 1515 *Shoal Waters* sailed through the open bridge and into the shelter of Havengore Creek and enjoyed more wonderful sailing through the myriad of creeks until just below the town of Rochford in the River Roach, when the tide turned. I followed it back down

through Paglesham Reach to a drying mud anchorage at Crow Corner beside Monkton Quay on Foulness Island at 1755. It was just a
short while later at 1900 when she touched bottom once again, this
time to enjoy a classic Roach sunset.

Summer was here at last and the evening was a warm one. I lay
cosy on the sleeping bag reflecting on the day's sailing and didn't
get to sleep until after midnight. We were away again at 0405 on
Sunday setting a full suit of sails including the tops'l, and almost
scraped against the sea walls to keep in the shallows and ghost our
way over the last of the flood tide in the lightest of airs. By 0545
Holliwell Point was bearing across the port beam and by 0730 seas
were running at a fair ol' rate and lumpy too, near Swallowtail No.
2 buoy. The Spitway buoy slid past the port beam at 0800 followed
by the Gunfleet South buoy, where we made a heading northeast
at 0845 for a time to explore the south side of the wind farm and
ride out the last of the ebb. Winds had become light and variable
by 1055, the time when *Shoal Waters* slipped into the Spitway and
was heading northwest, and at 1330 she was inside Bradwell Creek
gently ambling along under a hot beating sun through tightly spaced
trot moorings, into St Lawrence Creek and up to my mooring in
Goldhanger Creek for 1530. Trip tally 110NM travelled over three
days cruising.

11

The Essex Sunshine Coast

AN AREA THAT WILL ALWAYS HAVE a special place in my heart is the Essex Sunshine Coast; I have so many fond memories from infancy to my late teens, when every spare moment was spent here with all of the family: cousins, uncles and aunts, parents and grandparents, who owned a seaside bungalow or caravan. This coast starts at the River Colne with its historic Cinque Port of Brightlingsea. On leaving the Colne and Point Clear, the small isolated community of Lee-Over-Sands can be seen just over the rising sand of Colne Point. Here is perhaps one of the remotest communities in all Essex; it has a small waterway called Ray Creek that takes you right into the heart of its 30 or so dwellings along Wall Street. Part of this area is a nature reserve where rare plant species as well as migratory birds can be found. Ruins and the old rail carts of a former sand barge jetty now haunt Ray Creek, but just beside it is an ideal mud anchorage that Jim Lawrence, in his gaff dinghy, and I in *Shoal Waters* had a wonderful sail up to, running our plates into the deep mud 'east coast style' and downing sails for a chat and a cuppa.

After Colne Point and St Osyth Beach, the tide continues to take you seaward, up a fabled waterway known as the Wallet. For millennia its brown sandy waters have ebbed and flowed between the shore and Gunfleet Sands, and only in recent times have men built a

Georgian houses at Walton-on-the-Naze

Shoal Waters anchored by Walton Pier

vast modern wind farm, changing the once unobstructed and evocative seascape for generations to come.

Now traditional seaside towns such as Seawick, Jaywick and Clacton-On-Sea come into view. These towns once saw sailing barges quietly landing on their beaches, lowering sails to deliver the raw material for the building of their foundations. Now there are caravans, bungalows, beach huts and Art Deco buildings, broad promenades with colourful flower beds set in manicured gardens that are a picture in full bloom. All this is protected from the south-easterly gales that once smashed these shores by the building of groynes which also protect the beautiful sandy beaches.

Martello Towers abound on this stretch of coast. They were built to repel Napoleon's forces, but today the circular brick structures are wondered at by armies of holiday makers, who come to these accessible shores from big cities and towns such as London, a mere 50-odd miles away.

Passing Clacton pier the sailor comes to realise that the soothing sound of the seabird is exchanged for the joyous screams of merry funfair riders echoing across the waves. Behind the screams the ringing of arcades is heard, followed by wafting smells of salt-and-vinegar soaked chips filling the cockpit, causing you to swallow anxiously to a sudden hunger.

A south-westerly wind soon moves your little boat and the sounds become distant. Again seabirds can be heard and the skies are as wide and as high as you are likely to find anywhere in England. Like most of Essex, for every busy place there are a dozen quieter; soon Holland-on-Sea, with its little sailing club, named Clacton-On-Sea SC, and greens of mown grass to picnic on, comes into view. Take a compass bearing from Ro Mast and Frinton is found. After checking the mainsheet cleat, a look through a pair of 7x50s shows the spec-

tacle of battling kids settling scores over who has the biggest buck-
ets and fattest spades, while parents lay sunbathing beside wooden
wave breakers that span the wide widths of the flatland beaches that
were the favourite of Victorians at low tide. Above the beaches kite-
boarders fly the endless lawns. Behind them an isolated tower block
gives a handful of residents the most magnificent views across the
North Sea.

Walton-On-The-Naze appears soon after. Another pier and a
feeling you are in the very heart of unassuming England. Brightly
coloured beach huts nestle in the cliffs, and along promenades where
bedding plants are tended, the wide beaches have ample room to lay
striped deck chairs to sit in and drink tea. The Georgians liked it
here so much they built a model of their London streets in the form
of a row of three story terraced housing.

At 86 feet high the Grade Two listed Naze Tower has been
in view for a while but now gives a fine bearing to take you into
the sailor's playground of Pennyhole Bay—but not before you
head inland to scrape your keel while you take a closer look at
the Jurassic Naze cliffs which are registered as a Site of Special
Scientific Interest. These cliffs are packed with fossils, so are of
interest to seasoned or budding archaeological explorers and walkers, who can also stroll along the Crag Walk. The Tower was built
in the eighteenth century to aid navigation, being used as a bearing marker for ships entering the busy port of Harwich. Although
now a stone's throw from the eroded cliffs, it was originally a
quarter of a mile inland.

Dovercourt with its high lighthouse inhabits the coast north-
wards toward the deepwater haven of Harwich and the River Stour.
Further up the Stour, maritime towns such as Manningtree and
Mistley can be reached.

In the Walton Backwaters a myriad of inter-tidal creeks are to be found, which formed the backdrop for Arthur Ransome's tale *Secret Water*. For some sailors spending a night at anchor in the enchanted Hamford Water or Landermere Creek—in fact any of these creeks—can seem like playing a living part in the story.

For the cruising sailor who takes his views from the sea, the Essex Sunshine Coast can appear an unassuming coastline, one that is unpretentious in appearance; yes there are one or two unsightly blips but this stretch of coastline, the edge of the Tendring Peninsula, is packed full of historical and interesting places, just ripe for exploring.

Longshoring

THERE IS SOMETHING SPECIAL *about walking along a shoreline with your boat in tow. I call it 'longshoring,' not in its stevedore context but in that of* the ditch-and-marsh man or coast rambler who spends much of his time alongshore working his way in wild places.

One memorable walk with Shoal Waters in tow was on a foggy windless morning which precluded sailing. Ah, but I could still explore the shingle creeks that lay in the middle of my local river and just reachable two miles away. These are the two Collins Creeks where an ancient Saxon fish weir can be seen at low water springs. The flowing tide would take Shoal Waters there and I would walk as far as I was able the journey back. I drifted down the Blackwater and came to rest an hour before low water springs, and was amazed at how quickly I located the short stumps of the fish trap. Kneeling down I felt the line of soft wooden stakes that lay flat beneath a foot of clear water beside them. These were thinner timbers of three feet in length; below their spiked tops they were interwoven with even thinner lengths of wood approximately an inch in diameter and this would have possibly been the wooden netting.

I was connected to another time. It is highly likely this piece of wood has not been touched by man's hand since it was first worked by Saxon man over a thousand years ago, for fishing on an industrial scale, in part for human fuel for the gathering of sea salt from the nearby salt pans of that time.

The sun gleamed off the clear still water as it slowly made its return through the morning fog. I began to walk again along the fish trap, just keeping ahead of the slowly rising tide for a couple of miles. Shingle has banked up over many centuries, covering parts of the trap, but it remains a visible treat for the explorer.

The tide was now moving at a couple of knots, forming eddies as it raced between the slowly disappearing shoals of the two Collins Creeks. I was now in danger of losing Shoal Waters, so I set Cold Nose the hook and hopped aboard for a cuppa. I looked back down river and realised I had walked straight up the middle of a large part of the River Blackwater. Less than two hours later we were floating in eight feet of water.

12

In the Bawley

"WHO'S FOR TEA?" was the first call made by the skipper as we passed the tip of Maldon Promenade on our way downriver from Hythe Quay in a tender dinghy, and pulled alongside the clinker-built Gravesend bawley *Marigold*. "Oh yes" was the joint reply as warps passed over her bulwark and one by one we climbed aboard.

A teeth-chattering northerly had arrived just as we did, which had us all reaching for our top layers of clothing. I had come to join Kevin Finch, owner of *Marigold*, and a few other lads; together we would make a motley crew of seafarers out for a brisk winter sail. First there was Roger—the only man I know who began his life on a Thames barge as cook, to become mate and then skipper on the same vessel. Then there was Ben, usually at sea nine months of the year as part of a crew of seven sailing a square rigger, and last but not least Andy, a project manager on major tall ship rebuilds and other nautical projects.

The real treat for all of us was the lady herself, *Marigold*. She is a wooden boat of exceptional build quality; in fact her shapely timbers and fastenings ooze with a heritage that is from Cooks yard in Maldon where she was built in 1978. The yard has a long history in building and maintaining barges and working boats, and built *Marigold* replicating the lines of her sister ship *Lilian*, built in 1869, with an overall length of 30 feet, plus 14 feet of protruding bowsprit and a beam of 11 feet; her draft digs in at four feet six inches. She has a cutter rig and like *Lilian* she is engineless. In *Lilian*'s time there would have been a small fleet of her type of bawley based at an area called Bawley Bay which is in Gravesend on the Kent shore of the lower Thames. They were mainly shrimpers so would have been built with wet wells to keep the shrimps fresh, but they later adopted copper boilers in the main hold to cook the catch as soon as it was hauled up.

Kevin has been a skipper and mate on Thames spritsail barges so when he became owner of her three years ago he found both sailing and handling a pleasure, as in essence her bawley rig is very similar to that of the barge. She even has a forehorse for the staysail, and her mainsail can be fully brailed. *Marigold* had been kept at Brightlingsea by her previous owner for many years, so having her back in Maldon where she was built and where Kevin is based is a fitting homecoming for such a fine ship.

The Met Office weather forecast had given the promise of a Force 6 so one reef was put in while we waited for her to float. The time was two hours before high water and the aft section of her keel was still held firm in the Maldon brown stuff, but Kevin gave the nod to the foredeck crew and immediately her three-strand ropes were hauled on, sending her lengthy wooden gaff and six mast hoops aloft before her main canvas was brailed and left 'ready.' Next up was the staysail; this was already hanked-on therefore just needed the head block attached by its hook and then hauling up but 'backed to port'. The traveller was sent out along the bowsprit and the jib halyard pulled taught. Just as they are on a barge, most lines on *Marigold* are cleated but not hitched so they are ready to free off at a moment's notice. All was ready but a shift in wind left us in stays for a few tan-

talizing minutes, but it came back even stronger. We were now ready to get away, the nod was given and mainsail let out, the jib sheeted and all three sails filled in unison. The call was made to let go her mooring and we all looked and waited in anticipation for the moment she would shift. What happened next is a situation most east coast mud berth holders would be familiar with when aiming to get away early—she still clung dearly to the mud! Kevin asked everyone to move forward and then suddenly she responded and we began to shift, driving quietly forward in a glorious display of curved brown canvas that had her gunnel reaching water level until checked by her ballast bringing her on an even keel again. What followed was some thrilling winter sailing on the upper Blackwater, with plenty of time for everyone to either control the sheets or take a turn on the helm.

We had come along for a sail today but Kevin carries a full array of oyster dredges and trawling nets just as these vessels would have had in the golden age of 19th century working sail. *Marigold* is available for charter, for a whole day or for a few hours' taster on the top of the tide, to individuals or groups of up to six, and is a great opportunity for anyone who has always wanted to experience the thrill of a magnificent traditional East Coast working boat, be it a pure sailing adventure or practising those age old fishing methods.

← *The Gravesend Bawley* Marigold *on her mooring at Maldon*

13

Yantlet Creek

NEAP TIDES AND A PROMISE of glorious sunshine had my son Harry and I sat in Betsy, the pick-up truck, fully loaded the previous night with our 12ft home-built duck punt *Winkler* lashed down and secure. By 0500 we were cruising at 60mph round the M25 and high above the River Thames on the approach to the QEII Bridge toll booths at Dartford, Kent. Sailing under this bridge in *Shoal Waters* and looking up at this triumph of architecture from 'down there' is a wonderful experience, but then if you cross this bridge on a regular basis so too is having had your own minor triumph by being waved the £2.50 toll for making the crossing before 6am. We were lifted again on joining the A2, shortly after which we were greeted by a colourful sunrise climbing out from the horizon straight ahead.

A while later we had arrived at Allhallows and parked Betsy in Avery Way outside the *British Pilot* public house. Here we unloaded the punt and lashed her trolley astern and made our way to the end of the road where there is a padlocked five-bar gate. I lifted *Winkler*'s bow up onto the gate and with Harry on one side and me the other it was an easy manoeuvre to get her down again and carry on along the byway. The path cut across the centre of a field where cows roamed freely all around us. No matter how light a boat is, when it is being pulled a considerable distance overland like this it seems to treble in weight. *Winkler* was no exception and with her sailing rig, oars and other bits and pieces added my arms were beginning to ache. I had thought of a MkII trolley, after an earlier outing, with a wider axle that can be sited more amidships as this would transfer most weight on to the axle, but this would need more thought as it would then be too big to fit inside *Winkler*.

We had been walking for a third of a mile and had reached the other end of the field and the second of the two gates that have to be traversed before you come to the sea wall. This is a steep climb made easy by *Winkler*'s lightness, and anyhow I looked on this as part of the physical warm up for what was to follow. The remaining walk was along the level sea wall heading eastward into that blistering golden sun to the mouth of Yantlet Creek. It seems quite strange coming somewhere like this on foot and via road when I would otherwise come here by sea, but the seamarks Yantlet Beacon and London Stone which I could see clearly looked the same nevertheless.

The walk in total was approximately three-quarters of a mile to where I wheeled *Winkler* down on to an area of marsh and slipped her over the cant edge on to a six foot wide strip of sand. Here I raised her short yellow mast and hoisted her red lugsail. Harry wandered off to explore the creek from the sea wall.

The tidal waters of the Thames Estuary began lapping at *Winkler* as I pushed her out into deeper water and stepped aboard. Today's forecast was for south-westerly Force 4 to 5 and winds hadn't yet begun making themselves felt. Out over the estuary was a light mist that filled the air and masked the silhouettes of ships gliding in and out of this London River, their funnels just visible and with a slight lean aft that gave them a cheery, chin-up look about them.

Suddenly I felt the wind flowing around my ears and with a puff of wind *Winkler*'s sail filled and we were sailing. She accelerated at a brisk pace over Yantlet Flats toward Southend and where the ships were passing by. I threw my weight to port and dug her chine down deep. At the same time I set the short steering oar from her lee rowlock and let it trail along until I could feel it take bite. Her bow jutted to the left and back to the right in an erratic manner in response to my fumbling with the oar. Her mainsheet bound my fingers tightly as we rounded up and headed east toward the North Sea; we wouldn't be going that far though as the Yantlet Beacon now came abeam and I took a turn south and headed back inland toward the mouth of the creek.

The bay and creek lie in the lee of the predominant south-westerly winds and so make a most suitable area for gentle, unhurried punt cruising. The entrance is not well defined, and if viewed from a distance offshore is difficult to see, as it is almost closed off by a sand spit that has moved westward, leaving a mere 15 to 25 feet wide bottleneck at half-tide and where it is five feet deep an hour before high water neaps.

Winkler slid over the slack water of the bay with ease, then as we neared the creek the creeping trickle of a new flood increased its pace and became a mass of flowing swirls that gripped her firm and took us sharply around a hairpin bend where the salt water's eager pace slowed again to continue on its sinuous path more sedately. Immediately inside the creek a sluice gate with iron guard railings stands on the west bank. From here the creek heads further southwards into the low marshland of Hoo Peninsula where it broadens to an approximately 100 feet playground with level saltings on either side that are encased by an eight foot grassy sea wall. I grounded *Winkler* half a dozen times along the fringes here, but closer to the gut of the creek I picked out the wind shifts and tacked a way upstream. The depth remains at most around five feet hereabouts, and as *Winkler*'s oar trailed along behind in clear water her boom end clipped the sea aster on the lip of the marsh. We ran a steady course along its edge until we passed remains of an old wharf on the east bank. We were now in the creek's upper reaches where the surface resembled a stagnant pond with a skim of flotsam; the marsh beside us was a riot of swaying yellow-wort flowers, wild and in their full glory.

MOD warning signs are placed along the sea wall on the east bank from here, as the land behind is part of a firing range. The view further ahead is dominated by the landmark chimney of Grain Power Station, now closed, and eight gas towers, but the overwhelming feeling I was getting in Yantlet Creek was one of solitude.

The wind had by now built in strength, driving little *Winkler* further until the creek's width had whittled down to 15 feet again, and I held a course into the right of two channels where the creek forks. I had entered into a five feet wide rill which had lower banks that were topped by fleshy mattresses of marsh samphire. I'd never before seen this edible plant displaying such a frenzy of succulent green. The salty plant draped its chunky stems over the thick ooze on either side and I licked my lips at the thought of gathering some of it to go with this evening's supper. *Winkler*'s size had come into its own in this ridiculously thin rill as she carried on sailing, bumping from side to side as each swell of the rising tide threw us further into it.

We carried on in a stop-start fashion for the few hundred yards further ahead of us until we had reached the end of navigable water, and the sea wall where a sluice gate cuts off the creek.

Before the sea wall was built the creek continued into what is now a fresh water stretch, and once joined Colemouth Creek and the River Medway, completely encircling the Isle of Grain. It was then a haven for 17th century smugglers, whose contraband included casks of whisky or rum, called tubs, and who were often chased through here by the Revenue men.

In earlier times an arched bridge is thought to have spanned the creek. Its archway was built just big enough to allow barges to pass but over time maintenance was neglected and the bridge perished. This just may have been the time when the causeway was formed. Boats using the creek to cut through to the River Thames or into the Medway had to be dragged over the causeway if the tide was low. A court case in 1824 had a man on trial for clearing the roadway that crossed from the Isle of Grain to Stoke on the mainland. In doing so the public's right of way was obstructed more so than it already was by the twice daily covering of the tide. The man was found guilty by a jury.

The Isle of Grain today is securely connected to the mainland by the main A228 Grain Road and a series of dams and sea walls that have reclaimed much of the marsh, as well as protecting the area from ever-rising sea levels. The final commemoration stone was laid here in 1986, a year after the raising of the Thames Flood defences was completed.

Cattle can sometimes be seen roaming freely around the salt-marsh directly beside the creek, and because of this the marsh is deeply rutted by hoofprints which can trip the unwary explorer. While tucked up in the smooth waters of the creek my view northwards across the Isle of Grain marshes toward the Thames was often of ships coming to and from the river, and appearing to float on a green sea. The sail back down the creek over the last of the flood was truly magical with *Winkler*'s lugsail sporting a wondrous 'full' twist.

Harry reappeared from over the sea wall and waved us on. If it were not for the lee of the sea wall *Winkler* would be over-canvassed and quite possibly overturned, but I held on tight as she ran like a train all the way through a mile of glorious creek and out through its mouth—which had doubled in size, the time now being just after high water—and into the wide vista of the mighty Thames Estuary. Yantlet Creek had rewarded us with one of the most delightful punting jaunts I had had this year—a magical sail in a magical place.

A common irony for many creeks is that a backdrop of heavy industry ensure their solitude, and effectiveness as a haven for wildlife. Yantlet Creek is one of them.

14

Old Ways

SATURDAY DAWNED OVERCAST and the weather broadcast on the radio declared "light winds" would follow throughout the day. A little later that same day sailmaker Steve Hall and I were heading down Main Road after leaving the A14 in Suffolk. We had passed Fox's Marina and hugged the River Orwell coastline below that engineering wonder the Orwell Bridge. We were heading for one of the river's most delightful nooks, Pin Mill, for a day's fishing in the Leigh shrimper *Victorious*. I had helped move her up here a few weeks previous from the River Blackwater, when the trip took roughly five hours of motoring in a smooth sea.

How easy it can be to get up the Wallet if you are able to motor. This was not something I had the option to do during earlier attempts in *Shoal Waters* when I had to turn back off Clacton Pier after the favourable tide turned and wind died, wiping out any hope of nipping across Pennyhole Bay and taking the flood into Harwich, This happened while trying to sail up here on two separate occasions, one of them just days before.

As well as her purring Lister diesel engine that never misses a beat *Victorious* is fitted with an original working boiler that is used to cook any shrimps that are caught with nets in the traditional way. I was gasping for a cuppa half way up the Wallet and had crept down into the fo'c'sle but could not get the ship's stove to light. I tried and tried and then shouted up for help when suddenly Steve pulled up a bucket of sea water and in no time at all the ships kettle was sitting in the great boiler heating up our drinking water for a hot cup of tea! As we entered Harwich Steve guided *Victorious* alongside the pontoon where Gus, who had also lent a hand, and I were treated to a bacon sandwich too at Harwich's Halfpenny Pier. We were soon off again though, and in no time had shot the beam trawl for a drift along the River Stour, for a chance at supper. A few crabs, a couple of fry and a lot of jelly fish were reward for our efforts, but we were practising the old ways and that is what mattered to us. Just as there is when I go cruising, there is always a start and an end of a journey but it is not the final destination that is the be all and end all but the actual journey itself is where one really wants to be.

Gus, a bawley man himself, who owns and sails *Gladys*, also a former Leigh fishing boat, and runs Harry King and Sons Boatyard, had given us one of the deep water swinging moorings on the outside row at Pin Mill, and the following weekend we slipped the dinghy in beside the *Butt and Oyster* pub and rowed out to *Victorious* and climbed aboard. We prepared her for the day ahead before letting go her mooring line and moving into the Orwell's main channel. For this trip we trawled along the shelf of the north shore of Buttermans Bay, mostly under sail, setting just the boomless mainsail to drive at a snail's pace against the incoming tide. Steve suggested we remove the tiller from the rudder stock to steer by an age old method of adjusting the trawl warps: bring the bow line of the trawl warp aft and she would point up, let it forward and she would come beam-on. This is perhaps the essence of sailing a working boat and how privileged I was to be practising this art again in such a classic fishing boat as the *Victorious*.

Leigh Shrimper *Victorious* on her mooring at Pin Mill

On *Victorious*—paying out the trawl warp

We were sailing in its truest sense but in a different way and probably not as one would normally associate with going for a cruise. We trawled for a couple of hours more and then decided it was time to begin hauling. Motor-powered winches have taken over this task on modern trawlers—however, hauling the net by hand was, and still is for some, a physically hard way to earn a bob or two. We wrestled the net on board and while doing so I couldn't help humming the old shanty song 'Haul Away Joe' and with the cod end finally on the deck I then stood clinging to it and breathing all too quickly. It is sobering to know that for the professional fisherman who found his net is empty it would go back in and be hauled up all over again—no joke when you have bills to pay and mouths to feed. We were merely playing though, just like the thousands of pleasure boaters that make up the majority of people on the water. For us an empty net or not we would be going home happy. And we did.

And then another great day—even the stove worked in the fo'c'sle and an abundance of tea was flowing, served up 1950s fisherman style in white tin mugs. What more does a man need or want than to set a small sail and enjoy a cheerful brew? Tugging the dinghy along the Grindle a little later I was truly worn out, but in my head I was already planning the following day's action in *Shoal Waters*. On the way home we drove into Wolverstone Marina and had a cream tea and scones on board the sailing barge *Victor* courtesy of Wez, her skipper. With her canvas set *Victor* is a wonderful sight that can often be seen gliding along the River Orwell with day trippers on board and her tops'l fluttering in the breeze. After saying our goodbyes I headed down the A12 to Goldhanger, eagerly checking the radio for a forecast, to prepare the boat for an 0200 departure. This time I was even more determined to get up the Wallet.

15

Johnny All Alone

IT WAS VERY DARK WHEN I LET GO the mooring line in the early hours of the morning. In fact it was pitch black and I could not make out a thing; even so, I managed to bob and weave around shoal and through narrow sea from Goldhanger Creek to the Bench Head using my little ship's hugely oversized World War II landing craft compass without any mishap. As I made way north east up the choppy waters of the Wallet the new dawn broke out of the sea ahead of me into a glorious spectacle of light.

In a physical sense I was sailing alone but for one reason or another today I had Mr Negative sitting on my left shoulder and Mr Gung Ho Positive on my right. Between the three of us all manner of scenarios were being visualized but one niggle I just couldn't shake off was the thought of giant container ships piling in and out of Harwich and *Shoal Waters* somehow becoming stranded in the shipping channel with no wind; a very rational thought and one that may forever hang in the subconscious of the engineless cruiser. At this moment it was a negative one that unchecked could build and prey on the mind of the singlehanded sailor. I consoled myself that I had cut my teeth in engineless cruising by sailing the busiest shipping waterway on the East Coast, the tidal River Thames, and I had adapted my mind-set to what is perhaps the pre-emptive way of thinking needed to meet the challenges of cruising in this way.

The small auxiliary that I had carried in my first season with *Shoal Waters* had been intentionally left ashore, along with its bracket that was fixed to the transom, when I made the decision to cruise in the Thames Estuary under sail power alone—well, with the odd push and shove too—so it could no longer be an option if ever I was becalmed in such a situation. Cruising in this way, achieving a fair passage while alone and under sail power, was gratifying too and I thrived on the purity each mile the boat travelled gave, and the closeness with nature I had begun to feel.

I passed the seaside town of Clacton and in an hour Walton Pier was abeam before I could see the white shed at Harwich Harbour which gives a good bearing to aim north across Pennyhole Bay, by which time the new flood would lead me the rest of the way in, and to the mouth of the River Stour. A ship passed creating a tidal wave in its wake but *Shoal Waters* rode the choppy sea—sailing gallantly on, into Harwich Harbour, blown by a steady westerly breeze until I arrived at the green Ganges buoy where I took a turn to port and sailed back and forth in the mouth of the River Stour, where much mud is revealed at half-tide.

This broad estuary divides Essex on its southern bank from Suffolk to the north, and is a place where the trees come down to the sea. I took some time to admire the new surroundings and the busy goings-on across the harbour at Felixstowe Docks where cranes clanged noisily as they moved pile after pile of metal containers. I went about and hove to by the Ganges buoy and pondered at this spot where the training vessel was once moored. The 84 gun HMS *Ganges* spent seven years here, from 1899 to 1906. By that time a shore-based HMS Ganges establishment was built nearby and the ship was towed away. For training the mast of HMS *Agincourt* was erected and it was this tall mast with square yards which now stood erect a few hundred yards away on the Shotley shore, poking above the trees just beside the marina. After a few moments I sailed off, heading west but keeping into shallow water on the north side of the Stour, and began combing the contour of the shoreline. As I did so I pored over my Ordnance Survey map, which is always a great help for inshore cruising.

There it was, Johnny All Alone Creek. I pinpointed it on the map where it had hardly any resemblance to a creek with a channel, but the name was as charming as, and far more intriguing to me than, the Mistley or Wrabness I already knew, at the head of the estuary. No, I had decided I was going to spend the night at Johnny All Alone Creek so I sailed further northward and made a turn west to hug the margins of the Suffolk shore which by now were covering with the new flood, and then cruised past Admiralty Pier and Bristol Pier followed by Cockle Creek and Gibbon Creek, both silted gutways, and then Erwarton Bay's salting-fringed Waterhouse Creek. I was almost there—just a promontory of land to pass at Ness Quay which was the last of the East Coast quays used by the farm barges which, amongst other things, traded straw to feed London's horses for the 'London Mixture' they produced.

I pressed on with the wind still in my favour and passed close to the south cardinal that marks it and suddenly I could pick out my destination in a slight bay where I noticed a sluice gate. Sluice gates can be a tell-tale sign of a former creek, as they were sited at many which were cut off by the building of the sea wall. I had located Johnny All Alone Creek so I headed toward the shore and into barely two feet of water—this was as far in as *Shoal Waters* could comfortably stay afloat. There was no channel to speak of for it has almost completely eroded, but some saltmarsh still buffered the western edge up to the sea wall and a few trees and some low scrub decorated the

Entering the Harwich Rivers—Felixstowe container port ahead

Johnny All Alone Creek

tideline to the east. Beyond the sluices the creek reaches right up to
Beaumont Hall. Victorian sailing barges once pulled in here, owned
by the Wrinch family, local farmers who ran their own fleet and used
the creek right up until 1947.

In many ways the Stour is similar to the Blackwater: it is a broad
river and half of it dries at low tide, there is an ancient town at its
navigable limit, and there are ample places like Johnny All Alone to
dry out and spend a contented night on firm mud. As has happened
over time with other creeks names can change; Johnny All Alone
Creek was known as Erwarton Creek until sometime in the early
19th century when a fisherman named Johnny Shilling lived here
'all alone.'

It was now high water and time to position *Shoal Waters* to dry
out for the night. As in the Blackwater, the River Stour and its creeks
have many stumps laying around from old farm wharves or ancient
fish traps. I hadn't recce'd the creek closely beforehand therefore
any potential dangerous obstacles that may be protruding from an
otherwise soft muddy sea bed I could not see. I also did not want
to end up lying awkwardly over the gut of the creek, and I aimed
to leave about an hour after high water in the morning. This called
for a ferocious few minutes with the sounding cane jabbing, waving,
prodding and sweeping all around the boat, until I was happy we
were in a clear spot and then dropped *Shoal Waters'* 17lb fisherman
type anchor over the bow and dropped back a little before giving a
good tug on the chain to set the hook. From the stern I chucked in
the ship's small grapnel that I carry for just this type of calm water
scenario. I could then pull her stern round a little to miss the gut of
the creek, and within an hour and a half she touched bottom and
settled level with just the right amount of forward and aft sloping
that would allow, if one so chose, sleep without a pillow. As the

tide trickled away curlews moved in en masse across the mudflats and began working the tidelines for supper. For mine I placed an unopened can of Fray Bentos steak and kidney pudding in the kettle, half-filled with water, and boiled it for the usual three periods of six minutes, leaving ten minutes between each of the six; they recommend piercing the lid and boiling for 45 minutes continuously but my method saves on gas. I have to use the pliers to get the can out again as it is boiling hot but the pudding is deliciously cooked every time, especially with the added wafts of salt, mud and seaweed in the surrounding air. Soon afterward the canopy of darkness fell over us and as I slid down into the bag for a sound night's sleep; only the haunting call of the curlew could be heard echoing around the Stour under a twinkle of East Coast stars.

Sea Wall and Borrow Dyke

WHETHER GOING DOWN TO THE SEA or walking ashore from it, for those on the East Coast it is highly likely that an interaction with the sea wall will take place. There are hundreds of miles of it, an established part of the low-lying coastal landscape. Some walls are as high as 20 feet from ground level, yet we may hardly take notice as we traverse them going about our daily lives. Built from a variety of materials, the sea wall can appear as a functional barrier between us and the sea; it is a hard-edged, industrial-looking concrete mass in its crudest form; or a repeated pattern of preformed concrete tiles bedded and jointed with tar as is that classic Kentish rag stone walling; or the softer, more subtle affair that is a green and grassy mound hardly noticeable as it blends into the surrounding farmland. In seaside towns we use the wall as an extension to the street pavement and in low Essex and Kent marshland there is mile after mile of it that has been built to reclaim land from the sea for farming, or to protect areas such as Foulness or Canvey which were inundated, with great loss of life, in the storm of 1953.

The majority of the sea walls, particularly in rural areas, have been built using clay that was dug from the land just beside it. This has resulted in mile after mile of dykes, 'borrow dykes' as they are known, that sit just inside. Naturally filled with fresh water these are used to drain agricultural land and they also have sluice gates at intervals which allow us to control the flow of water through the wall into the sea. The borrow dykes sit tantalisingly close to the sea yet they resemble narrow, stillwater canals and have become a haven for wildlife, supporting reed warbler, shelduck, cuckoo, heron, swan and wood pigeon. Favourite shore birds such as the oystercatcher reside just feet away, on the other side of the wall, and are rarely seen here. In the fresh waters of the borrow dykes are eels and frogs, and insects and mice burrow and hide where foxes prowl along the edges.

16

A Hidden Backwater

FOR THOSE WITH AN AMPHIBIOUS CALLING The Walton Backwaters, a designated Site of Special Scientific Interest in north-east Essex, are a haven. An enchanting, seemingly endless watery world of small creeks, rills, nooks and old wharves all set in rural splendour. As the last of the tide trickles away from the far corners of the lonely marshes that make up this haven, what is left becomes a gurgling expanse of exposed mud where curlew, egret and redshank wade in search of a meal, and seals are sat high on muddy ledges to peer contentedly down onto the depths below.

A serene calm is then cast over the empty creeks; a stillness and quiet habitually broken by the striking call of an oystercatcher as it swoops low, tracing the final path of a retreating sea through the maze of shallows engraved into the now silver mudflats. Granted a sunny day, the views at low tide across the Backwaters are truly beautiful, but it is at high tide when the full potential of this cruising area is realised, as sea water touches the perimeter of approximately nine square miles and every wrinkle that holds water can be reached in a small boat. Like south-east Essex, the skies are big and blend in harmony with the sea. Saltmarsh is found in abundance here too and lines most of the creeks up to, what is for the most part, a raised sea wall, and beyond it the mainly arable land gently rises.

The view from inside the Backwaters toward the south-east includes the Naze Tower, an ancient navigation mark that overlooks the sea from the crumbling 70 feet high Naze cliffs, which has been converted to accommodate a museum with art gallery, tea shop and at the very top of the tower, a viewing platform. If we look to the north, clear of Harwich, giant cranes of Felixstowe docks can be seen in the distance, and as much of the Backwaters dries there is another common scene throughout, that of a yacht leaning to one side on a dry mud mooring, a picture that captures the charm and allure of simple East Coast cruising; although for many yachtsmen home is one of the numerous small craft moorings in the main channels, or the marina that retains water at all states of tide.

A visit to the Walton Backwaters in my cruiser can involve taking a route that Lord Nelson once took in his ship HMS *Medusa* in 1801, four years before, on board HMS *Victory*, he led a fleet of 27 warships to Britain's greatest sea victory at Trafalgar. While on a passage to the port of Harwich he dropped anchor outside it in shallow water, just off the Walton Backwaters, in what became known as the Medusa Channel.

Smaller craft may take a short cut and scrape over Pye Sand after low tide, negotiating what is then a tighter channel into Hamford Water before an advance can be made on the new flood up one of the many smaller waterways, such as Walton Channel, The Twizzle, Dardanelles, Oakley or Kirby Creeks. One may choose to round one of the many islands such as Horsey, Hedge End or New Island and have a try at heading up one of the lesser creeks with salty and enticing names like Boat, Barge or Cormorant Creek.

However, for the roof-rack sailor there is a back door into this playground that can be found approximately three miles inland from the North Sea in the Tendring district parish of Beaumont-Cum-

Moze, and at the bottom of Quay Lane: the delightful Beaumont
Quay. The land around the quay is privately owned, but the quay,
which is disused, belongs to Essex County Council, and though entrance is barred by a five bar gate, public access is, to use the words
of an English legend, through 'a gate that hangs well and hinders
none,' in this case a pedestrian swing gate beside it that just happens
to be wide enough to wheel my duck punt *Winkler* through.

I get a sense of going back in time when coming here, but what really excites me most is sliding *Winkler* over the stones of old London
Bridge, which spanned the Thames for over 600 years until being
demolished in 1831 and purchased by the then quay owners, Guy's
Hospital in London, to build the quay in 1832. They are probably in
as good a condition today as when they were first laid in London in
the 12th century, and they give entrance to the Backwaters through
just over half a mile of hand-dug canal called Beaumont Cut. This
somewhat forgotten corner of the Backwaters is exceptional in ac-
commodating a pleasant top-of-tide punt cruise in an area that has
barely changed for centuries. The depth of the cut from the very
bottom to the top of the quay stones measures four and a half feet
and there are usually a couple of feet of water in the cut when I ar-
rive here to launch *Winkler*, around two hours before high tide.

With a fine sailing breeze, waders on, back pressed to the sole
board and feet hanging over the gunwale, the straight run down
Beaumont Cut is not only a thrilling journey back in time but takes
on new interest as you round into Landermere Creek. From here the
fun continues as you can either dabble with the ducks by keeping going through the openings in the marsh round to Moze Creek and the
Old Moze Dock, or spread your wings further still. The Backwaters
are one of those places where you can find a sheltered area to linger
in a small open dinghy, even in the harshest of winds.

Duck punt Winkler *at Beaumont Quay* →

One example of this was last time I launched *Winkler* at Beaumont Quay. The weather was blowing up a fresh Force 4 southerly on a cold December morning and my hands were beginning to resemble two chunks of frozen gammon as I held on to the steering oar trying to trim her balanced lugsail. Together we managed to have a fantastic time in the area down to Gull Cottages, on the south side of Landermere Creek, where there is a small bay at Landermere Quay, which is not publicly accessible by car, but is itself a charming and tranquil hideaway set in idyllic punt cruising territory.

The cottages are Grade II listed and named after Sir William Gull, who was born the son of a humble barge owner and went on to become a physician to Queen Victoria. One of them was once a public house where one of Gull's associates, a giant of a man at over eight feet tall, would regularly stand outside and shake hands with residents above as they looked out from the upper dormer windows.

When I have sailed down here via the cut I have counted up to 60 wigeon and mallard duck take flight and watched every other wader made temporarily homeless when most of the saltings cover. *Winkler* then revels in the uncharted acres where there is plenty of wavy marsh-grass for her to sail through in four or five inches of sea. If the wind dies in such shallows leaving me becalmed I revert to other traditional punting methods rarely used in today's laid-back form of duck punt cruising. This requires lying in the prone position and using 'sprits,' two short lengths of cane, or in the same laying position using two 'paddles' the size of table tennis bats to propel us along for short distances. This is a very enjoyable form of punting that can get you up surprisingly close to photograph any seabirds that might still be cackling on top of the saltings.

The challenge is then to cruise back up the winding creek, which involves tackling a series of s-bends, exploring every nook as you go. In doing so you soon realise the difficulties faced by those early trading vessels trying to get up to Beaumont Quay, and how relieved they must have been when the more efficient, straight-line cut we see today was hand-dug by the Dutch to accommodate the beam of Thames sailing barges. For sailing vessels there is one danger to look out for halfway along both the cut and the snaking section of Landermere Creek beside it: this is an overhead power cable that hangs low, hindering entrance to normal yachts that have tall, fixed masts, but is not a problem for *Winkler*'s short rig. For the inquisitive skipper there is lots more to explore too, as back at the very top of Beaumont Cut sits the hulk remains of spritsail barge *Rose*; she was built by John Howard of Maldon in 1880 and spent her working life plying the shallow waters of the Thames Estuary, both under sail and later as a lighter barge, until being laid to the shelter of the cut and turned into a houseboat sometime during the 1960s; she's been slowly blending into the marsh ever since. There were three barges that worked out of Beaumont and though *Rose* wasn't one of them her presence here today sets the scene nicely.

There is evidence Romans gathered salt here too, as they did in many of the marsh-fringed estuaries on England's East Coast, and just east past the last stone of the quay is an old lime kiln of circular brick construction that was built in 1869 and which is veiled under a mound of grass. The kiln is of national importance, being the last remaining of its type, and together with the quay, and the brick building beside it that was used to store the lime, was scheduled a historic monument in 2003. Lime has been used as an ingredient in mortar since Roman times but there was huge demand for it back in the 19th century, both for use as a mortar additive and in agriculture. Consequently cargo barges were busily coming and going from this little port, not only to collect lime and farm produce but to deliver manure from London's congested horse traffic for the surrounding fields, and also coal needed to fire the kiln.

Time has stood still here to preserve a glimpse of what a rural Victorian farm port would have been like nearly 200 years ago in the age of commercial sail-driven boats. But above all, when the exploratory sailing is done, the Backwaters are a place to relax, and what better way to do it than to dwell among the saltings in a boat on a dreamy summer's day reading a favourite book—Arthur Ransome's *Secret Water* perhaps?

17

To Butley Creek

Shoal Waters was 50 years old in 2013, slightly older than me. She had been cruising all around the Thames Estuary before I was born and I still wonder if I may have unknowingly watched her pass by from one of the beaches, from Point Clear up to Walton, where I used to play as a child. Our cherished acquaintance however was now in its third year, and I had learnt her wrinkles and nuances and loved her dearly. Having settled into cruising her on the set of tide and the fickleness of the wind, a quest for coastal adventure drew me back up to the rolling countryside of Suffolk, a distance of 37 nautical miles from my mooring, to where I had targeted Butley Creek, also known as Butley River, a tributary of the River Ore situated at the very northern limit on my Imray chart of the Thames Estuary.

We left Goldhanger Creek at 1100 on Friday 5 July. High water was at 1138 that morning and I had hoisted the tops'l while on the mooring, as there was a very slight breeze coming in from the southwest I could make use of. *Shoal Waters* crabbed away across the freshly-covered ooze of The Stumble, slipping ever closer toward the north-east shore of Osea Island. By 1200 a working breeze came in from the south-east and by 1350 I found myself having to heave to in the lee of Wymark's Beach, at the mouth of the River Blackwater, to take in the tops'l, as the wind had by now built to a Force 4.

I passed Clacton pier in glorious sunshine at 1601 and slipped by Walton Pier two hours later as the wind backed and had noticeably decreased in strength to south-east Force 3. By 2010 *Shoal Waters'* pace had slowed to 1.8 knots as we crossed the Harwich shipping lane near the Outer Ridge port hand buoy. I experienced some nervous momentary lulls during the 30 minutes it took to make the short crossing, however we stayed clear of ships and passed west of Platters from where I could maintain a heading of 30 degrees northwards toward the River Deben. At 2105 Roughs Tower was bearing 125 degrees to starboard, and a few moments later I caught first sight of Woodbridge Haven ahead, off the starboard bow. While we were out of danger from passing ships, being just north of Felixstowe, we now had one lobster pot after another tripping us up. They seemed to be everywhere I pointed the bow. As luck would have it I could lift the centreplate and rudder to shake them off, but as darkness fell we carried on bumping into them for a while still until we had got past the impeding Knolls that crowd the River Deben entrance.

It had been a warm day earlier on but as the red sun sank beneath the horizon behind us we entered the magic hour of dusk and darkness fell over us. I had to wrap up again with woollen hat and fleeces to keep warm. North of the mouth of the River Deben I kept close to the shore where we crept along making 1 knot of boat speed over the ground. I was enjoying the sail so much I carried on to cover as much distance as possible. The sea-state had smoothed over, the wind now quiet and hardly noticeable. I could hear waves gently lapping on the beach by the short Bawdsey Cliffs, just north of Bawdsey Manor, and the distant rumble of a ships engine as it toddled out to the depths of the North Sea echoed for miles around.

Pressing on, we edged further up this lonely strip of coast until 0130 when my herding instinct took over and I decided to drop anchor in 10 feet of water opposite an isolated row of conifers that my night vision could just make out on the Bawdsey shore. We were in open water but when conditions are right, as they had been being so calm, I like to take full advantage of little anchorages like this that have served us well in the past. I put the anchor light up and climbed straight down into the warmth of the cabin. *Shoal Waters* swung restlessly to her anchor for the few hours we spent there. Her chain grated every once in a while and as I lay in the bunk tired and about to doze off I hoped for a decent breeze in the morning, for this was much needed to negotiate a safe passage through the tyranny of giant sand shoals and moving shingle bars that awaited us two miles further north at the mouth of the River Ore.

Daylight had me awake at 0430 on Saturday. I clambered out into the cockpit to be greeted by a magnificent dawn. The wind I had hoped for was missing but being optimistic I set the sails and paddled around for a while, to have a feel as it were. We were so close to the Ore entrance and yet it felt so far away. With a fair tide I would have attempted to paddle into the river, but it wasn't going to happen today. I could see the Orford Haven and Oxley Buoys quite clearly, and further north, the Orfordness lighthouse was sat on a narrow strip of shingle quite unique to the area. Its towering structure, painted in classic red and white stripes, sat to the west of a huge orange sun bursting out of the sea into the new day. The coast is slowly eroding on this part of England therefore Trinity House, who owned the lighthouse, had to make the difficult decision to close it down. The light had been turned off just the week before, after being in operation since 1792, a loss to those of us who go to sea for pleasure and for professional mariners alike. However, while it still stands the tower remains a decent bearing point during daylight hours;

what remains of its future is now in the hands of new owners the Orfordness Lighthouse Company.

The 0520 shipping forecast on Radio 4 gave a promising wind of north-east Force 3 to 4. This hadn't yet materialised and I'd been swift in setting the anchor again, as we were being taken south by the flood tide. The time was 0615 and I noted our position was bearing 315 degrees off of the third Martello Tower south of four which decorated the misty coast, up to what appears to be a quarantined row of quaint white-painted houses at Shingle Street. These delightful little homes sit on the lip of the North Sea; their chimneys stand above the pitched and tiled roofs and play peek a boo with the sailor who cruises close to the steep-to wall of shingle that they stand behind.

High Water today at the bar was at 1104 and preferably I wanted to be near the bar around low water so I could have a good look at how things were situated. As it turned out we had to wait at anchor another couple of hours and I was pleased to be in a position south, well away from the mangle of the shoals. I grabbed another hour's sleep until the knocking call of *Shoal Waters*' burgee reverberating through the mast and into the cabin woke me at 0800. The wind had finally arrived as forecast.

Watching the shoals appear as the falling tide weaves around them, descending ever deeper between the mountainous humps, is a wonderful experience, but at high water these obstacles become invisible and potentially deadly to vessels entering or leaving the river, so they demand respect. There is a narrow channel inside of the South Shoal and if the wind had stayed in the south this would have been an option, but the wind direction backing north had put paid to any attempt at this route. I couldn't wait to get among the lumps in the seascape and pass into the Ore, and was relieved that at last a

Houses play peek-a-boo at Shingle Street

In the River Ore

working breeze meant I could sail offshore to tack around the South
Shoal and pick out a line to sail into the river on a broad reach.

A face rinse in cold water, awake and alert with a stomach full of
eggs and bacon, and I was underway again. By 0900 I had steered
past the Oxley Buoy, a red can, and *Shoal Waters* was heading 330
degrees between two shoals. Helped by the generous flow of the incoming tide, we streamed along. I could see the sea-currents rush-
ing through any gaps in the shoals, all heading in the same direction
as we were, toward the confined channel of the Ore where every
drop of water headed northwards. We then entered this cauldron
where all the sea's forces converged. I had lifted the centreplate
to the halfway position to be well clear of the sandbar but I hadn't
expected the battering it took against the wooden casing as it was
bumped by vortex forces of H_2O colliding beneath us. It was all
I could do to try and steer her until past the inner Weir Buoy, a
green starboard mark, and then harden up into the main body of
deeper river. Then I lowered the plate fully and set about making a
succession of tacks.

I held one hand tightly to the tiller and played the sheets with
the other. I tried all I could to control *Shoal Waters* and hang on to
a level of steerageway. I guessed that for the short time we were
on a port tack, heading eastward with the bow pointing across the
racing set of tide, ferry-gliding as it is known, we were sailing at a
boat speed of 1 knot through the water, while simultaneously our
course over the ground was northwards (sideways) moving at an
estimated four knots. I could sail close to the steep-to shingle on
the east bank, which was a saving grace, but heaven help us if we
missed a tack. On a starboard tack, our theoretical making tack,
I guessed our boat speed over the ground to be 8 knots or there
about. I caught a fleeting glance as we rushed passed the delightful

Barthorp's Creek where birds topped a line of posts, and then a couple of World War II pill-boxes flashed past.

There were two other boats close by now, one was coming up behind us and the other had overtaken earlier at the Oxley Buoy, both having motored into the river. I hoped they would keep clear as, for now at least, we raced through Long Reach and I had limited control over the boat while going forwards beam first. We were at the mercy of the forces of nature. Thankfully the wind had by now built to a workable Force 4 and was freely coming straight off the sea from Orford Beach, that golden strip of shingle that is topped by green seablite and is unobstructed by trees or buildings, and on the starboard tack I could just manoeuvre *Shoal Waters* close to the west bank, where from the surface movement it appeared the tide was running appreciably slower. We were on a rollercoaster of a ride that was fraught with danger but I felt I was handling the boat well under the circumstances, and I was enjoying the moment. In truth this was fantastic, adrenalin-raising fun.

Fast-flowing sections of rivers like this can be likened to the revolving belt of a running machine. If a person were to attempt to walk across it their feet would be taken from under them and they'd probably be thrown off the end of it. Around spring tides when the river flows quickest the Ore can be a natural watery conveyer belt that happens to be a few miles long and we were to an extent quite happy playing on it.

Havergate Island, an RSPB nature reserve, loomed towards us and I turned north off the main Ore into a stretch of water that flows around its north bank known as the Gull. Its name is appropriate as gulls screamed deafeningly all around us. The opening to Butley Creek lay on my port side but from my angle of view in the cockpit I couldn't see it yet. Suddenly we were in shallow water and I took

Boyton Dock

Approaching the Butley Foot-Ferry

a reading with the cane and was pleased I could feel good ol' mud again. This was a mud horse that extends quite a way into the river from the west bank. I met it head-on but a lift to half plate and a push on the tiller pointed us back into free water until we could slide around it, and there it was, the entrance to Butley Creek. Moments later we had passed through an imaginary doorway.

The high tension we had endured coming through the Ore vanished. Now, obliged by a quartering wind, I settled back to soak up the new surroundings and rode the joint favourite of a fair wind and tide for all it was worth. I came across an anchored motor cruiser, I guessed it was between 40 and 50ft long, whose occupants were sat in deckchairs sunbathing on the flybridge two storeys up. I was genuinely surprised to see such a huge boat in a relatively small creek. They both noticed *Shoal Waters* sails and realised we were sailing up the creek. As we slid under their port bow I said hello and was intrigued enough to ask how long they would be staying. I could no longer see the couple's faces as *Shoal Waters* slipped along beneath them and passed clear of their stern. "We've been here all week and we might stay for another" was his cheerful reply. I can't dispute the beauty of the creek so who could blame him, he'd found an idyllic spot where their boat could stay afloat free of mooring charges, bar the wildlife they had no noisy neighbours, and from their high vantage point they had 360 degree panoramic views of some of Suffolk's most glorious sea-country.

When tidal creek and river estuaries are at low to half tide a greater part of the potential sailing area is gone, which makes sailing around any moorings or anchored craft, who understandably like to stay where the water is, a delicate business. There were a couple more yachts at anchor in mid-channel that I had to make sure we avoided. This is more of a problem when there is no wind, and I checked the paddle was to hand just in case. We were literally inches away as we glided past the brick ruins of Boyton Dock, a disused landing place, set in peaceful marshland, where coal was once delivered from up north and barges once lowered down to collect bricks. The ever-pacing tide seemed to slow a little now, and the breeze calmed too as we turned a corner and headed north. *Shoal Waters* moved persistently deeper into this arm of the sea where egrets and curlews plodded about on mud ledges either side of the creek, which would soon be covered up to the vivid lilac hues of sea lavender on the buff saltmarsh that caps them.

We passed close to the wooden post marking the end of Butley Ferry jetty. One of these stands on each side of the creek. This ancient ferry crossing is one of the lesser-known delights of the East Coast and has been in operation since the 16th century when it would have saved a walk of five miles for the nearest villagers to reach the larger village of Orford. Today volunteers operate this tiniest of ferries, one of four in the county, the others being Walberswick, Harwich and Bawdsey, and they can be seen wearing the traditional wide-brimmed hats that were popular with local agricultural workers and Butley ferrymen in the 19th century, as they convey their typical customers of today, the ramblers, bird watchers and cyclists enjoying the outdoors.

A few more craft swung to buoys a little further up, and as I passed them the sun beamed on to the green terraces that shaped the higher ground, and a deeper valley ahead. From where I was placed this gave me a fairy-story impression that the creek fell away and down into a deep valley beyond. It was now filling and every corner of mud was being covered with what remained of the new flood. It was widening too but was deceptively very shallow and each turn becoming more tortuous. Any advances I made toward the salting-fringed banks were thwarted by sticky mud. The deeper gut of the creek had vanished and I had no way of telling where best to sail other than by my senses of sight and feel. What followed was an attritional battle of wills, with me having to draw on all my waterman skills to gain ground and entry to this cavernous creek valley. The centreplate was hauled up and then released again. Each time we become stuck I grabbed the quant pole and pushed us back to free water, and off we would move again, bumping our way inch by inch along the creek in barely enough water to float. High tide was due in 10 minutes and although across a flank of swaying reeds I could clearly see Butley Mills, near the head of the creek, we wouldn't have enough water to reach it on this tide. I was content with the journey we had made as we had come a long way in 24 hours to be where we were now, far up Butley Creek, and our reward was to be alone enjoying the delights of a secret world where everywhere around us birds sang. I chose to anchor in a position near a remote farm quay and lowered *Shoal Waters'* gaff sail and placed a tin of new potatoes in the kettle to heat them. We would be dining *al fresco* deep in the beautiful Suffolk countryside.